From
STAFF ROOM
— *to* —
CLASSROOM II

This book is dedicated to my little brother, Kevin.
His curiosity guided his learning,
His heart inspired his passions,
His humor brought everyone together,
And we feel the hurt of his passing to this day.
Brian (and Robin)

From STAFF ROOM *to* CLASSROOM II

The One-Minute Professional Development Planner

BRIAN M. PETE ◆ ROBIN J. FOGARTY

CORWIN
A SAGE Company

For information:

Corwin
A SAGE Company
2455 Teller Road
Thousand Oaks, California 91320
(800) 233-9936
Fax: (800) 417-2466
www.corwinpress.com

SAGE India Pvt. Ltd.
B 1/I 1 Mohan Cooperative
   Industrial Area
Mathura Road, New Delhi 110 044
India

SAGE Ltd.
1 Oliver's Yard
55 City Road
London EC1Y 1SP
United Kingdom

SAGE Asia-Pacific Pte. Ltd.
33 Pekin Street #02-01
Far East Square
Singapore 048763

Printed in the United States of America.

Library of Congress Cataloging-in-Publication Data

Pete, Brian M.
From staff room to classroom II: the one-minute professional development planner / Brian M. Pete and Robin J. Fogarty.
   p. cm.
Includes bibliographical references and index.
ISBN 978-1-4129-7499-8 (pbk. : alk. paper)
   1. Teachers—In-service training—United States. 2. Career development—United States. I. Fogarty, Robin J. II. Title.

LB1731.P48 2010
370.71'55—dc22   2009023356

This book is printed on acid-free paper.

09   10   11   12   13   10 9 8 7 6 5 4 3 2 1

Acquisitions Editor:	Hudson Perigo
Editorial Assistant:	Lesley K. Blake
Production Editor:	Cassandra Margaret Seibel
Copy Editor:	Jenifer Dill
Typesetter:	C&M Digitals (P) Ltd.
Proofreader:	Theresa Kay
Indexer:	Jean Casalegno
Cover Designer:	Michael Dubowe

Contents

Acknowledgments

COLLEGIAL CONVERSATIONS WITH COLLEAGUES—"SHOP TALK"

Working with adult learners takes all the skill and grace one can muster—not to mention fortitude, persistence, and patience. The authors want to extend a warm and heartfelt thank you to the many colleagues who have shared their expertise and their many strategies over the years in order to make their work with adult learners successful.

As with many of us, it is often hard to remember the exact moment a strategy was learned; yet some of those encounters are crystal clear in our minds. We have made a few of those memories public in this acknowledgment in order to illustrate the power of collegial conversations and reflective practices.

For all others named here, our collaborations with you have definitely contributed to our bag of professional "tricks of the trade" as presenters, and facilitators, and coaches—even if we have not nailed the exact moment of inspiration, that "aha moment" that many of us feel whenever we talk shop. Here is the list of those whom we owe much well-earned respect, gracious gratitude, and thanks.

Jim Bellanca—Mrs. Potter's Questions and many, many more processing ideas

Valerie Gregory—Cooperative Learning Tear Share on the way to Albuquerque, NM

Kay Burke—Standards, Checklists, and Rubrics in Perth, WA, AU

Carolyn Chapman—The Multiple Intelligences Brain in Williamsburg, VA

R. Bruce Williams—Card-Storming at Skylight Training in Arlington Heights, IL

Susan Augustine—Heart-Healthy, Brain Smart Thinking in Palatine, IL

Donna Wilson—at a conference, Atlanta, GA

Marcus Conyers—Brain Foods in Lake Tahoe, CA

Mary Ellen Kotz—Mentoring Dialogue Strategies in Dover, DE

Beth Swartz—Cooperative Learning post card in Sochi, Former USSR

Terry Perry—Yellow Brick Road in Bloomington, IN

Gayle Gregory—Emotional Intelligence in Vancouver, BC, CAN

David Lazear—Multiple Intelligences Grid in Rosemont, IL

Teri Stirling—Higher Order Thinking Skills at Loyola University, Chicago, IL

Molly Moynahan—Photo Story at ASCD Presentation in Orlando, FL

Christie Ahrens—Leadership Skills in Chicago, IL

Jay McTighe—Enduring Learnings in Baltimore, MD

Carol Ann Tomlinson—Differentiation Strategies for Gifted in Melbourne, VIC, AU

Elaine Brownlow—Publishing Madness in Melbourne, VIC, AU

Tom and Patty Keaton—One Minute Write in Santa Fe, NM

Gene Kerns—Informative Assessment Responders in Dallas, TX

Laurie Kagan—Three Musketeers in Portland, OR

Cynthia Nesselroade—Menu of Coaching Services in Upshur County, WV

Judy Stoehr—Integrating Music into the PD Scene in Chicago, IL

Cathy Sambo-Duncan—Data-Savvy, Techno-Savvy Analyses in Kane County, IL

Art Costa—Three Levels of Questions, now, The Three Story Intellect in Honolulu, HI

Debra Pickering—AB Pyramid Game in Anaheim, CA

Linda Roth—Aha! Oh, No! in Palatine, IL

Bena Kallick—Picture Books as Metaphors (Leo the Late Bloomer) in Rosemont, IL

COLLEGIAL CONVERSATIONS WITH COLLEAGUES—"SPONTANEOUS SHARING"

In uncountable cases, participants have shared their own ideas with us, piggybacking on the strategies we were using at the time. They jumped up and said, "Do you know the one about . . . ?" and invariably they had a dynamite rendition of an active, engaging strategy to add to our ever-growing repertoire. To these "PD warriors," we want to express our appreciation and thanks for their genuine participation and the grand gift of strategies that we can use immediately.

If the earlier list of contributors was difficult to remember, this list is almost impossible to peg because in many cases, we did not even know the names of the teachers who shared so generously with us. Yet we almost always learn from the groups we are working with as they honor us with their expertise and wisdom about the teaching and learning process.

To all of the wonderful past and future participants, we thank you from the bottom of our hearts. We have learned so much from you and always look forward to those serendipitous moments in our trainings, workshops, and conference sessions when someone special will offer an idea to take away with us. Here is a very sketchy and very partial list of some of those memorable moments. Each has given us such marvelous ideas that they have become part and parcel of our professional work with adults. We owe you our gratitude.

The Little Book Foldable—Sixth-grade teacher in District 27, Queens, NY

Twelve Brain Principles—"Memory Pegs," Teaching Round in Palatine, IL

Texting as an IT Tool—Auckland, NZ

Energizers—Lovin' It, Good Job, Roller Coaster (to name a few) in Anytown, USA

Moveable Human Graph—Literacy Coaches in Clovis, NM

Reader's Theater Coaches' Story—AU Rules Football in Melbourne, AU

Letter of Commitment—Summer Training in Evanston, IL

Teach Less, Learn More—Curriculum Integration Teams' Reflections in Singapore

Parking Lot—Coaching Session in Venice, FL

Classroom Scenarios Video Tapes—Utrecht, The Netherlands

List/Sort/Label—Renaissance Learning T of T in Dallas, TX

Line Up Lanes—Coaching Seminar in Portland, OR

Professional Reflection Through Journaling—Buffalo, NY

Nursery Rhymes as Metaphors—Adelaide, SA, AU

PACTS (Paraphrase, Affirm, Clarify, Test Options, Sense Tone)—Lake George, NY

About the Authors

 **Brian M. Pete** comes from a family of educators—college professors, school superintendents, teachers, and teachers of teachers. Through his roles as a producer of educational videos, a publisher of educational resources, and a trainer of teachers and leaders, Brian has a rich background in professional development. He brings both a depth of understanding about effective professional development experiences and a technical know-how for practical implementations.

As a founding partner of RFA: A Robin Fogarty Company, Brian has video recorded classroom teachers and professional experts in schools throughout the United States, Europe, Asia, Australia, and New Zealand. He has an eye for the teachable moment and the words to describe what he sees as skillful teaching and effective coaching. Brian's work on educational videos includes *Best Practices: Classroom Management* and *Best Practices: Active Learning Classrooms.*

He has authored a number of resources: *Nine Best Practices That Make the Difference; Twelve Brain Principles That Make the Difference; Data! Dialogue! Decisions!; A Look at Transfer; The Adult Learner;* and *From Staff Room to Classroom: Planning and Coaching Professional Learning.* Brian has a bachelor of science from DePaul University of Chicago and is completing his thesis for his master's in fiction writing from Chicago's Columbia College. He and his co-author received the NSDC Book Award in 2006 for *From Staff Room to Classroom: A Guide for Planning and Coaching Professional Learning.*

Brian is currently the lead trainer in a major initiative in Singapore for the TLLM Ignite Schools. He brings his humor, wit, and charm to all of his professional development sessions.

Robin J. Fogarty is president of RFA: A Robin Fogarty Company, a Chicago-based, minority-owned educational publishing and consulting company. Robin received her doctorate in curriculum and human resource development from Loyola University of Chicago. A leading proponent of the thoughtful classroom, Robin has trained educators throughout the world in curriculum, instruction, and assessment strategies. She has taught at all levels, from kindergarten to college; served as an administrator; and consulted with state departments and ministries of education in the United States, Puerto Rico, Russia, Canada, Australia, New Zealand, Germany, Great Britain, Singapore, Korea, and the Netherlands.

Robin has published articles in *Educational Leadership, Phi Delta Kappan,* and the *Journal of Staff Development.* She is the author of numerous publications, including *Brain-Compatible Classrooms, Literacy Matters, Ten Things New Teachers Need to Succeed, How to Integrate the Curricula, The Adult Learner, A Look at Transfer, Close the Achievement Gap, Twelve Brain Principles, Nine Best Practices,* and *From Staff Room to Classroom: Planning and Coaching Professional Learning.*

Robin received her bachelor of arts in early childhood education at SUNY, Potsdam, NY, and her master's in instructional strategies from National Louis University in Evanston, IL. Her current projects include co-authoring a formative assessment book, cowriting a gifted education preschool curriculum, and the co-developing of *Response To Intervention PD,* in partnership with Renaissance Learning.

Robin is known as the teachers' teacher. She brings a wealth of knowledge and passion to all endeavors and is often complimented on her lively sense of humor and personable ways.

Introduction

PREMISE

Robin Fogarty and Brian Pete have conducted professional development with schools, districts, state agencies, and departments and ministries of education around the world. During that time, they have acquired a vast compendium of highly interactive and engaging strategies that get adult learners intensely involved in professional learning sessions. *From Staff Room to Classroom II: The One-Minute Professional Development Planner* presents these interactive strategies for others in the field to use in their work with adult learners.

PURPOSE

The glory of these gathered strategies is that they work just as well in the classroom setting as they do in the staff room setting. As educational participants experience these compelling strategies in the workshop setting, they are encouraged to embrace them and, eventually, to adapt them for use in the classroom. In essence, the staff developers, administrators, PLC teacher-leaders, and presenters of PD (professional development) model the very "lookfors" they want to see in the active, engaged, student-centered classrooms of today's quality schools.

CHAPTERS

The first four chapters are focused differently and present a total of 144 strategies, 36 in each chapter. They target four different intended audiences, all of whom are involved in staff development: staff developers; principals and assistant principals; Professional Learning Community leaders; and group facilitators. Chapter 5 presents sample applications for classroom teachers.

There are five chapters—including an introduction, the four main chapters, and a closing chapter. They are titled to depict the focus of the presentation or facilitation.

DESCRIPTION OF THE MORPH GRID FORMAT

The strategies are arranged in a matrix, or grid, called the Morphological Grid. This grid provides the framework for creative presentations that seem to *morph* by aligning forced choices or forced relationships. Each time one element is changed, the presentation takes on a new form or morphs into a different presentation format. The strategy comes from the Synectics Model of creative innovation that is used in business and industry to seek new and unique products (Osborn, 1963).

In brief, the morph grid consists of a bank of ideas that can be arranged and rearranged according to personal preference, team needs, or as a random act of creativity. The three categories in the grid relate to the three well-stated principles of an effective presentation:

1. Tell them what you are going to do! *Capture* the audience's attention!

2. Do it! *Captivate* them with the information!

3. Tell them what you did! *Close* with keepers!

These three principles are designated in the grid according to the following principles: Column 1—Capture, or "Openers"; Column 2—Captivate, or the "Meat of the Matter"; Column 3—Close or "Closers." Capture the audience's attention! Captivate them with information! Close with keepers!

Juxtaposed with the three columns are 12 interactive strategies placed horizontally, across the three columns. By selecting 1 item from the 12 in each column, the presentation takes shape. In essence, the selections plot the course of the presentation.

How the Morph Grids Work

For example, the presenter might begin with a selected strategy (for example, joke) as the opener to *capture* the attention of the group. Then, the presenter will *captivate* them with the meat of the matter, using another strategy (cooperative learning task), and finally, the presenter will *close* using a closer, or final strategy (reflection). This process becomes quite clear as one actually looks at a morph grid and sees the array of items possible for selection.

Openers	Meat of the Matter—Middles	Closers
1. Strategy 1a	Strategy 1b	Strategy 1c—Reflection
2. Strategy 2a—Joke	Strategy 2b	Strategy 2c
3. Strategy 3a	Strategy 3b	Strategy 3c
4. Strategy 4a	Strategy 4b—Cooperative Learning Task	Strategy 4c
5. Strategy 5a	Strategy 5b	Strategy 5c
6. Strategy 6a	Strategy 6b	Strategy 6c

It is said that creators of television comedies, dramatic series, and soap operas use a morph grid to keep the story line changing from episode to episode. Thus, when an entirely new plot line develops, often introducing new characters, the story line literally morphs into something quite different.

A final word on this Morph Grid is needed. Although the strategies are assigned to a column (opener, middle, closer), many of them are interchangeable with other columns. An opener in one case might be used as a closer in another presentation. It really is up to the creativity of the presenter and the risk-level she or he is willing to take.

How to Use Morph Grids Effectively

There are several options available for using the Morph Grids for the selection of items. Some provide random approaches for selecting items from the three columns, while others choose tools and techniques more deliberately.

Random choices are the preferred method. They often result in highly creative presentations. These random models, which use forced choices more often than not, take the presenter into new territory, using tools and techniques that are a bit out of the comfort zone. Yet on the other hand, the deliberate choice of items in the three columns may provide the presenter with the most appropriate tools for the target presentation. Using either random or deliberate selection methods, here are a few ideas for selecting various tools and techniques in order to mold a presentation.

Random Methods of Selection

1. Roll a set of dice and assign the numbers rolled to each column to make a group selection.

2. Use the last three digits of an individual's phone number and assign the appropriate numbers to the columns to select random items.

3. Use a deck of cards, 1 through 9 and Jack = 10, Queen = 11, King = 12, Ace = Free Choice.

4. Use the last three digits of an individual's Social Security number, or the first three digits of his or her birth date.

Deliberate Methods of Selection

5. Have the designated team leader choose a number for each column.

6. Have various team members select an idea for each column.

7. Follow the order sequentially, until all ideas have been used once.

8. Choose two favorites and one new strategy to move outside the comfort zone.

1

Morph Grid I

Presentation and Facilitation Strategies

Capture: Openers	Captivate: Middles	Close: Endings
1. Story (page 7)	1. PowerPoint (page 19)	1. Circle Back to Beginning (page 31)
2. Joke (page 8)	2. Role Play (page 20)	2. Key Points (page 32)
3. Quote (page 9)	3. Reader's Theater (page 21)	3. Take Away Item (page 33)
4. Cartoon (page 10)	4. CL Tear Share (page 22)	4. Reflective Lead-In or Stem (page 34)
5. Images (page 11)	5. Human Graph (page 23)	5. Action Step (page 35)
6. Film Clip (page 12)	6. The Three Musketeers (page 24)	6. Letter of Commitment (page 36)
7. Picture Book (page 13)	7. Magic Book (page 25)	7. 3-2-1 Reflect (page 37)
8. Music (page 14)	8. Step Book (page 26)	8. PMI—Plus! Minus! Interesting! (page 38)
9. TV Character (page 15)	9. Graphic Organizer (page 27)	9. Analogy (page 39)
10. Mystery (page 16)	10. Inner and Outer Circle (page 28)	10. Yellow Brick Road (page 40)
11. Lighting and Sound Effects (page 17)	11. Rhetorical Questions (page 29)	11. Dial 4-1-1 for Information (page 41)
12. Surprise Guest (page 18)	12. Woven Questions (page 30)	12. Aha! Oh, No! (page 42)

INTRODUCTION

Presenting professional development (PD) sessions is what staff developers do all day every day. They must plan, design, and execute their PD activities with skill and grace. They design all-day sessions, half-day sessions, one-hour sessions, and even 10- to 15-minute review sessions.

From Staff Room to Classroom II: The One-Minute Professional Development Planner is the perfect designer tool to create a quick plan for any of these professional development sessions.

DIRECTIONS

Roll a set of dice three times to select an activity for the three elements based on the numbers rolled. Be courageous and go with the actual numbers. Don't cheat. It will make your professional development lively, original, and effective.

1. *Capture* the participants' attention with openers.

2. *Captivate* them with the "meat of the matter."

3. *Close* with keepers.

CATEGORICAL LISTING OF ALL MORPH TOOLS

Check Appendix A for an index of strategies by type of tool (e.g., collaborative tool or management tool).

CREATIVE OPTIONS

Remember, the strategies are interchangeable and often work as any of the three elements, depending on the context and how they are used. An opener may be used as a closer or even as part of the meat of the session. Be creative and use the grid of strategies with your own creative flair.

MORPH GRID I: PRESENTATION AND FACILITATION

Capture Strategy 1. Story

Explanation (What it is!)

Tell a personal story to make a telling point. In other words, tell any story that comes to mind that seems related, relevant, and rich with innuendo and meaningful commentary. As soon as someone says, "I'm going to tell you a story," that person has the audience's attention. Everyone loves a story, and better yet, they remember the stories you tell. Stories follow a set pattern: They have a beginning, a middle, and an end. Stories are easy to listen to and easy to "take away." Stories that make a specific telling point are memorable and repeatable. In short, stories do, indeed, tell the story. In fact, they tell the story that sticks.

Application (When to use it!)

Don't hesitate to use a story as a surefire opener. Stories are one of the traditional tools in the toolbox of a great presenter. You can reference that story throughout the talk and effectively circle back to that story at the end of your talk.

Remember, a personal story is not an affidavit. Don't hesitate to borrow a story or to shape a story so that it makes a strong point and helps frame the topic of the session. Also, don't be afraid to ask participants to share their stories with you. Ask them to tell about an incident with a student that fits the topic focus, or ask them to tell a story with a partner. These are powerful moments in a presentation because stories help to personalize the learning and make a point in an intensely meaningful way.

Elaboration (How to use it!)

"Quality Teaching"

For example, tell the story of the best teacher you ever had as a way to lead into a discussion on quality teaching.

> The teacher I remember most is my fifth grade teacher, Mrs. Dockerty. Everyone thought she was mean, and none of us kids wanted to have her for fifth grade. But the secret that was revealed to her students was that she was a wonderfully kind and caring teacher who had the highest standards and the highest expectations for the students in her care. When they say, "Students don't care what you know, until they know you care," they are talking about Mrs. Dockerty. She cared about each and every one of us. She knew us as individuals. She knew that I loved art, so she put me in charge of the bulletin boards. I worked harder for Mrs. Dockerty than I did for any other teacher I ever had because I believed that she believed in me.

MORPH GRID I: PRESENTATION AND FACILITATION

Capture Strategy 2. Joke

Explanation (What it is!)

Some people say they aren't good at telling jokes, but maybe they haven't looked at it in the right way. When you hear a joke you like, try to tell it back to yourself—after you have stopped laughing. Repeat it several times so that it makes sense and you have the right words. Type the joke into an e-mail to make sure that you have it. Then, consider jokes you have heard, and try to put them into some kind of classification that could be valuable to you in the future. Have them ready to go.

Application (When to use it!)

The idea of opening with a joke is as old as time itself. Comedian or not, presenters use this strategy to ease their way into a relationship with the audience. The right joke, at the right time, presented in the right way, is a no brainer. It is a fail-safe way to get the audience on your side. This is an effective, telltale sign of a skillful presenter. The joke is on you if you cannot use this old favorite as part and parcel of your presentation repertoire. (Just kidding!)

Elaboration (How to use it!)

Tell an appropriate joke that emphasizes an idea.

When you want your staff to work as a team or to have a defined goal, use this:

Team Work

Two guys are on a steep staircase moving a very heavy piano. After an hour or so of sweat and struggle, the first guy says, "We will never get this thing up these stairs." The second guy says, "Up? I thought we were taking it down!"

This is an opening that works every time:

A Welcome

"Good morning everyone! I just wanted to share with you my understanding of our roles today. As I understand it, I'm supposed to talk and you're supposed to listen. If you finish before I do, let me know."

An opening remark, used with audiences of diverse cultural backgrounds:

A Multicultural Audience

You know what we call someone who speaks three languages? Trilingual.
You know what we call someone who speaks two languages? Bilingual.
You know what we call someone who speaks one language? American.

MORPH GRID I: PRESENTATION AND FACILITATION

Capture Strategy 3. Quote

Explanation (What it is!)

Use a memorable quotation to inspire and engage. An opening quote is a great way to start a presentation with a provocative thought. The quote often provides a philosophical backdrop for the content focus. It encapsulates what you are going to say, in elegant and poetic language. The quote is the message in a nutshell, and it carries with it the wisdom and respect of the author. By using a quote to make a telling point early in your presentation, you have set the stage for substance and truth. In addition, the use of the quote can be even more powerful if you have designed a way for the audience to process or think about the quote in a deliberate way.

Application (When to use it!)

The most appropriate time to use a quote is when you want to catch the attention of the group or when you want to put a punctuation point on the discussion. Quotes tend to stop us in our tracks. They make us take note—they make us stop, look, and listen, if you will. It can set the stage for what's to come, which is how we are using it in this context: to capture attention up front. Yet the right quote, sprinkled within the text of a talk, may be the pause you are looking for. Also, when the perfect quote is used at the end of a talk, it can put the topping on the sundae. Quotations are the secret spice that one adds to the main dish. They provide a delicate, yet distinctive flavor to the presentation.

Elaboration (How to use it!)

Professional Learning Initiative

"It is impossible for a man to learn what he thinks he already knows."

—Epictetus

Consider this quote, and then with a partner, answer these two questions:

1. How is this relevant to staff development?

2. What do you think you already know?

The Role of the Academic Coach

"Come to the edge," he said.

They said, "We are afraid."

"Come to the edge," he said.

They came.

He pushed them . . . and they flew.

—Apollinaire

MORPH GRID I: PRESENTATION AND FACILITATION

Capture Strategy 4. Cartoon

Explanation (What it is!)

Utilize a cartoon to *show* instead of *tell*. "A picture is worth a thousand words"; that's a lot of words! Why not find the perfect cartoon to make your point? A cartoon should be funny, and laugh-out-loud funny is the high bar. Yet even if the humor is a quiet "aha" connection, it adds value to your presentation. Some will walk away with that picture in their head. They will remember the visual more than the words. Try to find one-picture cartoon frames or a comic strip with few panels. *Far Side* cartoons are great as openers. Also, the *Phi Delta Kappan*, an academic journal, is filled with educational cartoons. *The New Yorker* magazine runs a bunch of great contemporary cartoons in every issue.

Application (When to use it!)

Why not use the raucous or subtle humor of a well-conceived cartoon to emphasize a key idea? Place it strategically in your presentation, so that it appears at just the right moment to stress a critical point. Show it right after an intense passage or after a controversial idea is presented. The cartoon moment relieves the tension and provides a needed release of emotions. Another idea about appropriate applications is to use the punch line as a way to make your point, and then return to the cartoon as you close the day. It makes an effective ending point.

Elaboration (How to use it!)

Teaching and Learning

There is a cartoon that speaks to the constructivist classroom and the idea of teaching and learning. In the cartoon, a boy tells his friend that he has taught Stripe, his dog, how to whistle. His friend says, "I don't hear him whistling." The boy replies, "I said I taught him. I didn't say he learned it." The following is a list of similar cartoons that might be used in a presentation.

Pour and Store Cartoon

Brain Works Cartoon

Nine Best Practices Cartoons

Twelve Brain Principles Cartoons

Capture Strategy 5. Images

Explanation (What it is!)

A picture or image can speak for the words you may say ad infinitum. But the picture or image often needs a setup to make the point crystal clear. Everyone may not draw the same conclusions from the image presented, so it is imperative that you illuminate the essence of the message. In short, make your memorable picture memorable! Make it such a powerful image that it becomes an indelible mark on the mind of those exposed to it. Make it speak to the audience in ways that enhance and embellish, engage and envelop. Images create a visual literacy that is just as much a part of the communication spectrum as speech itself.

Application (When to use it!)

A picture has as many uses as there are images in the universe. This picture can become part of the promotional materials before the event even takes place. It might be part of a brochure, a pamphlet, or even a faded image in the background of the notes. The image may be a thematic thread that runs through many aspects of the event.

In another way, the image may be used as a pivot point for introductory comments that set the stage for the rest of the activities. It might be a classic, like a rendition of the Mona Lisa, to open the discussion about the secrets to a highly functioning professional learning community (PLC).

Also, a final image may be the punctuation mark that you want to use as a culmination piece. In that way, that mental image is the last impression from the session and, perhaps, a lasting impression for the participants.

Elaboration (How to use it!)

One example of an image that makes a clear and concise point is a sketch of a three-story brownstone building to represent the metaphor of *The Three-Story Intellect*. The first story is about gathering facts, the second story is about analyzing information, and the third story is about application. To see this as a visual metaphor cements the idea in our minds that there are three levels of thinking or ways of thinking about ideas. Often, the image can be retrieved in our minds as an indelible picture that appears as a chunk of information. This is sometimes a more accessible memory piece than a set of words that convey a similar meaning.

MORPH GRID I: PRESENTATION AND FACILITATION

Capture Strategy 6. Film Clip

Explanation (What it is!)

There are many film clips from mainstream movies that illustrate a subject with more emotional impact than you could ever do with a well-given speech, or even with the visual aid of a PowerPoint presentation. Films speak to us. It is copyright legal to use short clips (5–8 minutes) from a video or DVD for classroom use. By selecting a short, succinct piece that makes a telling point, you set the stage for a robust discussion. In addition, you can create a mood and a tone to enhance the message you want to send. Also, you can introduce a powerful theme that will thread through the entire session and enrich the conversations and the discussion with a consistency and continuity that emphasizes key points. In brief, these film clips present memorable moments in your presentation.

Application (When to use it!)

A five- to eight-minute clip sets the tone and texture of the day. When selected with care and intent, the film clip becomes the centerpiece of the session. It acts like a magnet that attracts other elements of the presentation. Use the clip as a dramatic opening to further articulation and group discussion. The film clip opener is especially effective when shown on a very large screen, or on many screens if addressing a large audience. The figures take over the room, looming large with a commanding presence. Of course, films are appropriate for smaller groups too, where the discussion can be especially lively and personalized. On a side note, although this section is dedicated to *openers*, this specially selected five- to eight-minute film clip can also provide a dramatic endnote to a session. In fact, you might use it to open and close a session to create a dramatic circle-back effect.

Elaboration (How to use it!)

For example, on our Web site (www.robinfogarty.com), we have a list of clips to accompany the 10 chapters in the book, *Ten Things New Teachers Need to Succeed.* The clip from *Dead Poets Society* shows a scene that illustrates the power of setting high expectations for students; *Pay It Forward* has a wonderful performance task for middle-level kids; and *Mr. Holland's Opus* shows how teachers differentiate instruction to meet the talents and needs of every student. There is no end to the power of these film clips in professional development situations. Over time, you will accumulate a set of clips that are easily embedded in the electronic presentations. These favorites will become a standard part of your presentation repertoire.

MORPH GRID I: PRESENTATION AND FACILITATION

Capture Strategy 7. Picture Book

Explanation (What it is!)

Picture books provide a viable tool to lead into a sensitive issue, topic, or subject of concern. They offer simple words and illustrations that can zero in on an idea in a unique way. Picture books are timeless: Their message is accessible to all and they are universal in their appeal to our sensibilities. Think about the idea of timelessness. Picture books such as *The Very Hungry Caterpillar* (Carle, 1986), *The Polar Bear Express* (Van Allsburg, 1984), *The Five Chinese Brothers* (Bishop & Wiese, 1938), *Leo the Late Bloomer* (Kraus & Aruego, 1994), and *The Little Engine That Could* (Piper & Hauman, 1961) have withstood the test of time. They have no temporal boundary that would make them any less effective today than they were ten years ago. Their messages are accessible to all age groups, across the four generations of adult learners that need to be addressed in professional learning opportunities in schools throughout the country. The appeal of picture books is universal because their messages are universal. All can relate to the parental concern for *Leo the Late Bloomer* as they track his development in learning. Everyone can connect to the motivational message of *The Little Engine That Could*.

Application (When to use it!)

Use a picture book to frame the topic or set the sights of the audience in a metaphorical way. Use the language-deficient five Chinese brothers as a metaphor for English language learners, or use the hungry caterpillar to showcase a sequence of predictable ideas. Use *A Fine, Fine School* (Creech, 2001) to highlight a positive school climate, or use *If You're Riding a Horse and It Dies, Get Off* (Grant & Forsten, 1999) to signal the reluctance to change. Find just the right book to make your point, and the opening piece of your presentation will be remembered forever. Of course, you can thread the character and the theme throughout your presentation. Also, it may seem a bit risky, but sometimes a staged role play enhances the picture book reading.

Elaboration (How to use it!)

You might use the entire picture book *Click, Clack, Moo: Cows That Type* (Cronin & Lewin, 2001) to talk about the role of the negotiator in adult-learner situations. Or you might read the whole book aloud and even have the audience join in on the chorus. You might use part of the book *Through the Cracks* (Sollman, Emmons, & Paolini, 1994) to begin discussions about the achievement gap. You can then ask the participants to turn to a partner and name some of the kids who are falling through the cracks in their school. Another way to use the book is to take some digital pictures of the cover and several key pages and use that in your PowerPoint presentation to tell a summary of the story. The digital photos adapt easily to the electronic format and are powerful images to accompany your telling of the tale.

MORPH GRID I: PRESENTATION AND FACILITATION

Capture Strategy 8. Music

Explanation (What it is!)

Music is a presentation tool that is often overlooked. Music gets the attention of the participants in subtle or dramatic ways, depending on the selection and the purpose. It definitely invokes emotion in the audience. You might play marching music to get them upbeat and at attention, or you might play soft and soothing music to set a tone of congeniality and collegiality. You might use a song with lyrics that speak to the topic, or a regional song that depicts the locale or theme of the area. Music can be a backdrop or a focal point, depending on how it is used; in either case, when there is music in the room, everything feels different. On a side note, using music in the staff room also gives you the opportunity to discuss how and why music can be an effective tool in the classroom.

Application (When to use it!)

Open the session with a piece of music. Playing music at the beginning of the session, as people are entering the room, sets the mood for the day. It is a wonderful way to set a positive tone and elicit an emotional reaction at the start of the session. Use music in the background early in the session, as teams are working on tasks. To use music as often and as effectively as possible, you have to use it regularly. The more you experiment with it, the more applications you will find. The more you use music in your presentations, the more you will experience its impact. Music is a universal language, just as visual and performing arts are universal languages. Everyone is touched by the music and its uses are limitless once you have embraced music as a standard tool in your professional toolbox.

Elaboration (How to use it!)

For example, begin a session with a dramatic flair. Use a powerful, emotional piece of music that does more than set the mood. Consider a rousing Sousa march or a stadium rock and roll anthem that stirs peoples' souls and gets their hearts pumping. Or play some soothing jazz as people enter the room in order to create a setting for quiet conversations and personal connections. Use country music to honor the western region of the country where your presentation is taking place, or swing into the day with the blues as you prepare to speak in the south. Use the music of the country you are in to honor the hosts. In short, use music, music, music, to speak the languages of the world.

Capture Strategy 9. TV Character

Explanation (What it is!)

Using a television character to open your presentation is a device that elicits emotional connections through a feeling of familiarity. The character represents certain qualities, particular viewpoints, and predictable traits that provide an immediate comfort zone for the audience. The character you select may evoke instant laughter, a sarcastic snicker, or even a loveable "Ohhhh!" But whatever this TV character does, use it to provide a known context for the presentation message. The character represents the message, and in a way, becomes the messenger—literally carrying your message in a memorable way. Use a familiar character from a television show to make a point. Start with a character whose personality traits are well known and easily recognized. For example, use the Archie Bunker character making an outrageously biased remark to open your presentation on reliable sources in the media. Showcase this character and wait for the reaction. Then, make your point clear.

Application (When to use it!)

Consider starting a session with just the image of a TV character on the screen and asking the question, How might this character answer the following question? Or use the character as a mascot of sorts, to represent and emphasize your viewpoint. Use the character to depict an opposing viewpoint to provide contrast and constructive controversy. Make the character the voice in the room that says what everyone is thinking but is too afraid to say out loud. You can also let the character close the session, if that seems appropriate. It makes a nice set of bookends for the presentation.

Elaboration (How to use it!)

For example, this idea came from a workshop presented by a school-based team on the subject of increasing parent involvement in parent-teacher conferences. On the stage was the teacher with slides of the archetypal parent, Homer Simpson. Using the character as a pivot point, participants predicted how he might react or interact in various situations. The session demonstrated, through humor, some of the issues that teachers face while conducting parent-teacher conferences. This provided the catalyst to discuss the changing parent roles and responsibilities for parent-teacher conferences.

MORPH GRID I: PRESENTATION AND FACILITATION

Capture Strategy 10. Mystery

Explanation (What it is!)

Opening with a mystery, brainteaser, or conundrum of sorts sets the tone that this professional development day will be challenging and fun. A mystery is always a grabber; it gets the group on their toes right away. A mystery or puzzler, or even a paradoxical statement, is a compelling opener because people usually stay tuned in until they get a solution or some insight into the situation. It's human nature. The brain loves a challenge and has a hard time letting go of it without some sense of satisfaction. To open with a splash, with impact, with an attraction that tugs at the mind, can be a powerful starting point for any presentation. In addition, as the group processes their problem-solving strategies, you have a chance to model good instructional behavior for the classroom.

Application (When to use it!)

Pose a mystery to hook the group at the very start of the presentation. Give them the set up as an early part of the opening piece, and then let them have fun with it. Let them mess around with the idea by encouraging partner or group collaborations. Then, sample the responses and help them unpack the thinking that led them to their conclusions. Give the answer at some point, or they will feel cheated. It's just the way it is. They want you to know that they know, but they also want the official confirmation of their successful thinking. It is possible to thread this idea of a mystery or teaser through the session by using other similar situations. In this way, the participants have some authentic practice with this mode of operation, and they become more confident and more skillful.

Elaboration (How to use it!)

There are plenty of such riddles available on the Web. Here is one we have used:

A man buys a horse for $50. He sells it for $60. He buys it back for $70. He sells it again for $80. Did he win, lose, or break even?

This is used to look at problem-solving strategies. Don't give the answer too soon. Let the group work on the problem. Let them have fun with it and stay with it long enough to feel a sense of accomplishment. Here are some Web sites to reference for riddles and puzzlers:

http://www.braingle.com

http://www.brainteaser-world.com

http://www.iriddler.com

http://www.brainbashers.com

Capture Strategy 11. Lighting and Sound Effects

Explanation (What it is!)

The technique of using sound effects or lighting techniques to open a performance is as old as theater itself. When Maya Angelou stepped into the laser-like spotlight on stage, the only sound was her voice singing hello in ten different languages, and a sudden hush fell over the audience. The effect was as dramatic as it was intended to be. That is the power of using lighting and sound as tools for opening a presentation. These are basic tools and techniques available to presenters, regardless of the setting. Whether on a large theater stage or in a small conference room, there are possibilities for manipulating the lights and for arranging sound effects. Lest you forget these two fundamental tools, think about a time, similar to the opening moments with Maya, when lighting and sound effects were so skillfully used that you remember that moment to this day.

Application (When to use it!)

Use lighting or sound effects to get their attention. Use bright lights that dim, dimmed lights that brighten, or spotlights that focus. Use the sound of your voice, or of another's voice. Use music in the background, or use a rising crescendo of music that drowns out all of the chatter and talk of the early arrivals. Use lighting and sound effects early in the morning or just before lunch. Use them right after lunch to signal the start up again, or use them to end the session with drama and flair. Use lighting and sound effects any time you want to transition or to create a punctuation mark in the presentation. Use lighting and sound effects as often and as naturally as you use your own voice and your reassured visuals.

Elaboration (How to use it!)

For example, imagine this opening:

The room goes dark, a low rumble is heard from the back of the room, and then the sound becomes clear. It's a train, a steam-powered locomotive that picks up speed. You can't see it but you can hear it. And then, on the screen, you see a pin light. Small at first, and then bigger and brighter . . . you think it may be the headlamp of the steaming train until you realize it's not a headlamp, but a rising sun, and the sound of the train blends into the sound of an orchestra of powerful strings that lift the sun. You have their attention. You have hooked them, and you are ready to make your opening point.

MORPH GRID I: PRESENTATION AND FACILITATION

Capture Strategy 12. Surprise Guest

Explanation (What it is!)

It is a ploy; it is a technique presenters use to cash in on the element of surprise. It creates a level of anticipation that is always welcomed when you have a message to deliver. This guest is your emissary and will deliver a parallel message that will illustrate your points in highly memorable ways. The presence of a special guest is not only motivating and exciting for the group, it also creates huge credibility for you and the work that you are doing because it illuminates your creativity and resourcefulness. Don't be fooled into thinking that the surprise guest has to be someone famous. You can invite anyone into the scene that will represent another voice in the message you want to share.

Application (When to use it!)

After your heartfelt opening story of a student who overcame all obstacles, you have the student walk in. You tell the story of a teacher who made a difference in your life and then the teacher comes out to join you. You confide in the audience that you have arranged for a surprise guest to open the session: a guest whom they all know, but have never met in person; a surprise guest who is famous and fabulous! After you build it up to the point of excited anticipation, you welcome a local sports hero, or newscaster, or weatherperson. Use this strategy at the beginning of your sessions to proclaim, in no uncertain terms, that future sessions with you as their presenter are going to be dynamic, unusual, and uniquely inspired.

Elaboration (How to use it!)

A guest speaker featured recently at a national conference was a young man who had learned the art and science of forensics. After being introduced by his forensics teacher, he proceeded to deliver a stunning and eloquent speech that clearly illustrated his skill and poise. After this opening, the audience was more than eager to hear from the teacher who had prepared this young man with such expertise. The speaker's credibility rose by 110% because he had demonstrated his skillfulness through the stunning results of his work with this student.

MORPH GRID I: PRESENTATION AND FACILITATION

Captivate Strategy 1. PowerPoint

Explanation (What it is!)

Microsoft's PowerPoint or Apple's Keynote, or other electronic presentation tools, provide the perfect platform for the "visual literacy" tools to accompany your "oral literacy" presentations. The opportunity for striking visuals—clip art, pictures, graphs, video clips, and digital photos of classroom examples or workshop examples—is endless. The parallel opportunity for stunning auditory literacy—sound effects, music, voices, quotes—is also endless. At the end of the day, the impact is limitless. Yet there are protocols for electronic presentation tools that guarantee quality applications of this powerful media tool. Never read the slide to the audience. The overriding rule: Use slides judiciously to track your talk.

Application (When to use it!)

Key things to remember when using PowerPoint:

- Limit the number of words on each slide. Ten well-chosen magnet words is the max!
- Use a bold, simple, and large font. Minimum font size should be 18pt; average font size is 40pt, to allow for easy reading from the back of the room.
- Fancy, exciting transitions are neither fancy nor exciting. Keep the production-level low and the content-level high.
- Try to come up with original background templates that fit the content and make your presentation look different right from the start.
- Choose a design template in which the words are easily distinguished from the background.
- Do not read the PowerPoint. Use key words as the pivot point for your talk.
- Use the PowerPoint to enhance the presentation, not as the presentation.

Elaboration (How to use it!)

An example of an effective PowerPoint presentation is one that provides verbiage and visuals in tandem to support the message or content. A presentation on data-driven instruction uses a graphic for a human graph activity about how data-savvy the participants think they are. Then clear, concise visuals are displayed, with one-word labels as cues to accompany the activity.

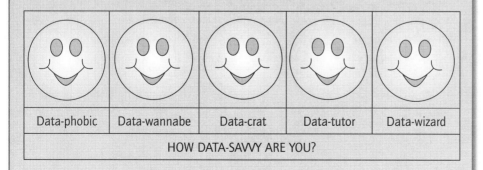

Data-phobic	Data-wannabe	Data-crat	Data-tutor	Data-wizard
HOW DATA-SAVVY ARE YOU?				

MORPH GRID I: PRESENTATION AND FACILITATION

Captivate Strategy 2. Role Play

Explanation (What it is!)

A scripted or unscripted role play is a powerful way to make a point. Select a situation that is key to the information you are presenting. The role play is effective because it involves people from the group, so they are totally invested in the activity. Others that are not directly involved in the activity are still interested and engaged because they are eager to see how it goes. Also, there is risk involved in this kind of improvised theater, especially when performed in front of peers. The energy is high, the attention focused, and the people chosen frequently surprise everyone with their laudable performances. It is even possible to do several similar scenarios that feature different people each time.

Application (When to use it!)

Orchestrate a role play to demonstrate and model an idea. Always find the "actors" before you begin the day in order to get their permission and give them clear directions so they will know what they are saying, what they are reacting to, and the point you are trying to make. Also, keep the role plays short; don't assume the "role players" will be able to carry on more than two or three minutes of a scene. But don't be afraid to facilitate this powerful strategy within the context of your presentation to exaggerate a point. It can be an opening or closing activity, of course, if you use it appropriately. There is something quite endearing about the group producing their own version of the scenario, and it can be used in small and large group settings.

Elaboration (How to use it!)

For example, you can use this technique in an adult learning situation by having a role play of a reluctant teacher at a workshop or of a teacher explaining a new lesson to an observing principal.

Or you can use student role plays. Have someone from the audience come up and play the role of a defiant student misbehaving in class or a student struggling to read informational text. One role play used for differentiation makes its point by having three students (tall, medium height, and short) attempt to reach prizes that have been placed at a certain level to represent the grade-level standards. Naturally, one reaches it easily (gifted), one reaches it with a little more effort and standing on tippy toes (average height), and the other (shortest) cannot reach it all, no matter how hard he tries. Then the presenter asks: "Do we lower the prize (standard) or give the kid a chair?" Thus, it makes the point of doing something differently to help every child succeed.

MORPH GRID I: PRESENTATION AND FACILITATION

Captivate Strategy 3. Reader's Theater

Explanation (What it is!)

Reader's Theater is an oral reading in which members read a role from a text or script in order to convey information through the activity. This works when summarizing a book or making an abstract concept into a more concrete example. Using a prepared script, or a piece simply divided into three sections, create a reading with two or three characters. In this way, their interactions illuminate and illustrate the gist of the book being summarized and help make the complex topic or idea more clear. It is one of those highly energizing activities that gets everyone involved because everyone, literally, has a role to play (or read). Do not hesitate to use this as a viable interaction as your workshop unfolds. It will be one of the most memorable moments of the day. In addition, some participants will be inspired to go back to the source and read more about the topic.

Application (When to use it!)

Again, this is a wonderful way to make an impact on participants in the course of sharing information in your workshop. While it is a simple piece, it needs some very specific logistical management. From experience, this seems to work well when you have the participants move their chairs away from the table, forming a circle—"knee to knee, eye to eye, head to head," as cooperative learning gurus often say. This removes any barriers between participants, and everyone is poised to read, listen, and discuss. Once the reading is done, allow time for the participants to debrief fully in small groups and also sample some ideas in the large group.

Elaboration (How to use it!)

For example, an original script created around the book *The Tipping Point* involves three archetypal characters and summarizes, in a scripted format, the key concepts of how change happens. Another Reader's Theater is orchestrated around a script about how three basketball coaches use data. It is called "The Coaches' Story" and has three coaches analyzing the game data and discussing how they can adjust their practices and goals based on the new and emerging data. It serves as a great example of how teachers can use data to inform their practice. These are just two examples; there are so many possibilities for this most powerful of strategies. One that comes to mind is a one-page information sheet on teen brains. It easily separates into three parts for a Reader's Theater. Think about a piece you use and how you might turn it into a Reader's Theater.

MORPH GRID I: PRESENTATION AND FACILITATION

Captivate Strategy 4. Cooperative Learning (CL) Tear Share

Explanation (What it is!)

The *Cooperative Learning Tear Share* activity is an all-involving team strategy that is used as a way to share information from a reading, viewing, or lecture. In selecting a brief and concise reading, and responding to key questions, the group is able to unpack the ideas, summarize them, and then have a more robust debriefing discussion. Similar to the cooperative learning jigsaw, the structure of this collaboration is more intense, with more investment from the members throughout the entire process. It is a powerful staff room technique that is facilitated for interactivity and teamwork.

Application (When to use it!)

All members read and write answers to the four questions, then they jigsaw summaries of each of the questions. In teams of four, number off 1, 2, 3, and 4. Each person has one 8½ × 11 sheet of paper, folded into fourths, with the corners numbered 1, 2, 3, and 4. In each corner, each person writes down one of the four questions from the board. The questions are related to the reading to follow. Then, all four members read an article or passage from a text (not too much reading, maybe three or four minutes). Each member of the group gives written answers to all four questions. When finished answering all four questions, the members tear the paper into four squares and pass all of the answers to Question 1 to Member 1 in the group, all the answers to Question 2 to Member 2 in the group, and so on.

Member 1 has four papers with answers to Question 1.

Member 2 has four papers with answers to Question 2.

Member 3 has four papers with answers to Question 3.

Member 4 has four papers with answers to Question 4.

At this point, all members take a minute to read over the answers to their designated question and then prepare an oral summary of the answers. When all members of the group are ready, Member 1 gives an oral summary of the four answers to Question 1. This continues until all have shared.

Elaboration (How to use it!)

For example, Shel Silverstein's poem "Smart" is a perfect generic piece to use to model the Tear Share activity. Participants read the poem, answer four higher-order questions (e.g., Agree or disagree with the title of the poem? or What inference can you make from the last line?), and then, doing a teaching round, summarize their group of answers for the others.

MORPH GRID I: PRESENTATION AND FACILITATION

Captivate Strategy 5. Human Graph

Explanation (What it is!)

This is a whole-class cooperative learning structure in which participants move to a corner of the room, take a stand on an issue, and stand on the imaginary axis line in order to create a "human bar graph." As participants take a stand on an issue along a continuum, they are expected to have an opinion or justification to support their stance. By sampling the various lines in the bar graph or the various corners in the scatter graph, points of view are revealed and exposed. As others give their views, people are able to move to another spot if they find themselves inspired by the comments they have heard. It is a dynamic graphing activity that elicits opposing ideas and, in the long run, lots of verbal volleys. The energy in the room is high during a human graph activity sharing.

Application (When to use it!)

The *Human Graph* can be used as a pre- or postlearning strategy, to stir up prior knowledge, or to check for understanding. It is also a highly effective strategy to use in the middle of the session to garner ownership from the participants on a critical issue. Participants often get very involved in this graphing activity, moving from spot to spot as various ideas come to the surface. Thus, it serves as a tool for interactivity, yet it offers a wonderful "breather," a pacing component in which participants get up and move in the midst of intensive input from the presenter.

Elaboration (How to use it!)

1. A simple example is this statement about quality teaching:

   "Teacher evaluation should be based on student achievement."

   Have the participants go to one side of the room if they agree and the other side if they disagree. Then, have them discuss with those next to them why they are there and explain their reasoning. Sample opinions from both sides of the room.

2. Another example, this time using five points on the graph, is this statement about the brain:

   "About the brain I know . . ."

Next to nothing	Not much	Don't know what I know	A little bit	A lot

This becomes a prior knowledge piece, giving the presenter valuable information on where the group is in terms of their knowledge-level on a given topic.

MORPH GRID I: PRESENTATION AND FACILITATION

Captivate Strategy 6. The Three Musketeers

Explanation (What it is!)

The Three Musketeers is known as the "teepee" grouping for sharing. In this activity, everyone stands up and raises one hand in the air as they find two other people to match up with. This is a quick and simple way to get your participants into cooperative groups for an easy sharing round on the topic of the day. This collaborative strategy works because it personalizes the ideas while, at the same time, limiting the interactions to three people—which makes the discussion more manageable. In addition, this grouping is done standing up, so it is an expedient way to get participants up and moving while not taking too much time out of the day. Participants share easily because there is safety in the small group.

Application (When to use it!)

It is a great activity to use when you want to sample the ideas of the people in the room as they connect to the topic at hand. It calls for personal opinions on and examples of the target idea and, at the same time, a sharing of these with the whole group after the early sharings in the smaller groups. This is often used as an opener in order to place focus on the key concept. It can also be used quite effectively as a closer in order to circle back to the issues under scrutiny. In any case, this cooperative learning strategy, introduced by Kagan Publishing, is a winner whenever it is employed.

Elaboration (How to use it!)

For example, one can use The Three Musketeers by saying, "After you introduce yourself to your two new partners, talk about one thing you know about teaching the adult learner." After a few minutes of discussion, get the attention of the room and have them sample some of the things they know for sure about the adult learner. Then proceed with affirming information about what they have identified correctly.

Another way to use The Three Musketeers strategy is with the idea of "closing the achievement gap," in which participants are asked to talk about who the kids are in their school who are falling through the cracks. Then a listing of the types of kids who are struggling is compiled. With these types of students clearly in their minds, the workshop information takes on very personalized meanings for the participants.

MORPH GRID I: PRESENTATION AND FACILITATION

Captivate Strategy 7. Magic Book

Explanation (What it is!)

The astonishing power of this foldable book is in its ability to stimulate higher-order thinking. It is the perfect tool for looking at both the big picture synthesis and the partial picture analysis. It is such a complex foldable that it can hold lots of information. Here are the directions:

1. Each person needs two single sheets of copy paper.

2. Fold the first sheet in half (hamburger style), and tear it in half.

3. Save one half and tear the other half in half again, making two strips of equal length and width. Save the two strips and put them aside.

4. Take the second whole sheet of paper and fold it in half (again, hamburger style).

5. Then, fold both sides back toward the crease, creating wings.

6. Grasp the middle section of the same piece of paper between the two wings.

7. Now, find two marked spots, for thirds, and tear through the fold to the mark. When you are done, they should look like three teeth or a tiara when you hold them up.

8. Now, open the torn paper, lay it flat like a mat, and weave the two strips through the sections on each side.

9. After the weaving is done, fold the book together with the six sections in the middle, giving it a good crease.

10. Carefully find the middle, and with your thumbs, tug the section open, revealing the six sections. Close it again.

11. Carefully find the two edges beneath the six-sectioned middle, and pull on the far edges. As you pull out, the pages flip and the big "magic" page emerges; the *Magic Book* is ready for the note taking activity.

Application (When to use it!)

Create the Magic Book foldable as described above, and use it throughout the heart of the workshop for participants to gather all of the information you want them to take away with them. It is such a handy application tool because it has the features needed to elaborate on an idea.

Elaboration (How to use it!)

Use the large section to solve math problems, and then turn to the six sections and analyze the problem-solving strategies used. Or use the six sections for parts of a story, and write a new ending on the large page, with an illustration to match.

MORPH GRID I: PRESENTATION AND FACILITATION

Captivate Strategy 8. Step Book

Explanation (What it is!)

The *Step Book* is a perfect and highly effective tool to delineate the key points that you want to emphasize. To make a Step Book, take two pieces of paper and fold them length-wise (hot dog fold). Tear along the fold so that you have four halves. Stack three half-sheets together, and then stagger them by half an inch. Fold it over almost in half, and you will see the other ends staggered. You will have six pages to your step book. Because of the steps, the items are literally lined up for easy access. This tool lends itself to six to eight items collected as a quick reference. This Step Book is sometimes called the Ladder Book because it looks like a ladder of sorts.

Application (When to use it!)

The Step Book is a viable technique to use in a workshop setting as you are unpacking a listing of items or tools for future use. For each item, you have provided a place to write notes or even make sketches as reminders of key points or critical aspects. Not only does this Step Book make an ideal note-taking tool, it also serves as a useful artifact for continual use when back onsite. This can also make a culminating activity, with the Step Book used to succinctly summarize the final points of the day.

Elaboration (How to use it!)

One example is to delineate the six traits of writing by making the six-page Step Book a reference tool for teachers to share with students. By labeling each page with one of the six traits (i.e., 1. Voice, 2. Ideas and content, 3. Sentence fluency, 4. Word choice, 5. Organization, and 6. Conventions) and noting the specific details of each one, teachers become clear on the content and, in turn, can share the very same booklet with their students.

Another example is to capture six to eight different kinds of journals to use with new teachers in mentoring programs, or to use with professional learning communities. Each journal type dictates a novel approach to the journaling. More specifically, the six journals include Dialogue Journals, Double Entry Journals, Action Journals, On a Scale of 1 to 10 Journals, Art Journals, and Letter Journals.

MORPH GRID I: PRESENTATION AND FACILITATION

Captivate Strategy 9. Graphic Organizer

Explanation (What it is!)

Use a graphic organizer, such as an attribute web, an analysis fishbone, or a concept map as a way to make the thinking visible. The graphic organizer literally helps to organize thoughts on paper. Graphic organizers, when used with cooperative groups, are best developed on chart paper so that everyone in the group can participate and contribute. The writing on the graphic organizer should be bold and large, creating an example of group work. Vary the types of graphic organizers used in professional development in order to model the uses for the classroom. Various organizers are used, depending on the learning goals and the information to be organized.

Application (When to use it!)

A graphic organizer activity is appropriate as a small group interaction during the professional development session. This activity gives participants time to make sense of the information by working together to organize it on a graphic chart. This might be comparing items with the use of a Venn diagram, sequencing ideas on a flow chart, or even brainstorming items on a concept map. The real power of these activities is in the discussion that ensues as the team tries to place items in their proper order or in the most appropriate place. While the completed chart is important to make the thinking clearly visible to all, it is really in the conversations that ideas are truly crystallized.

Elaboration (How to use it!)

For example, a web of ideas for a group brainstorm of possible topics for a professional learning community to address might include test data, exploring and examining student work activity, or even identifying and analyzing the needs of one student who seems to be struggling. Another example is to use the graphic organizer, called the *fishbone analysis,* to display information on a team goal, and all of the elements that will impact that goal, both positively and negatively. These are typical practices that call for graphic organizer activities. Using these graphic tools, saving them for "touchbacks," and reviewing them to track progress are all relevant ways to make them an ongoing part of the team work.

MORPH GRID I: PRESENTATION AND FACILITATION

Captivate Strategy 10. Inner and Outer Circle

Explanation (What it is!)

The *Inner and Outer Circle* is a whole-class cooperative learning strategy that engages the learner with movement, rhythm, song, and verbal interactions. Use an Inner and Outer Circle activity to debrief an issue or to unpack the depth of an idea presented earlier. To use this strategy, follow these steps:

- Have the participants form a big circle and then count off by twos.
- The ones take a couple steps into the circle to form their own inner circle.
- The twos tighten their circle to become the outer circle.
- The circles march in opposite directions, outer circle clockwise, inner circle counter clockwise. As they march, they sing a simple song (e.g., "Three Blind Mice," or "Row, Row, Row Your Boat"). When the music stops, each person in the inner circle matches up with someone on the outer circle to debrief on the selected topic.

Application (When to use it!)

While this is a high-energy activity that gets everyone laughing as they sing the silly song, it does provide a serious forum for one-on-one conversations. It can be used when you need a pacing piece to get participants up and moving during a presentation day. It provides the movement, the climate, and the dialogue that fosters genuine discussions that are often full of insights and wisdom. It is an opportune time for two people to go head-to-head on some ideas and to personalize the talk-through with their own stories, informed opinions, and individual thoughts. The circles often move twice, giving the participants two different partners to work with.

Elaboration (How to use it!)

One example of an Inner and Outer Circle discussion topic is "Tell about a coach you remember and what made this person so memorable." Another is to ask participants to "Share a good idea to engage a reluctant learner," or to "Tell one strategy you use to differentiate learning for the advanced learner." There is no end to the possibilities of what you can do in this wonderfully energizing activity. There are so many conversations that spark true insight into the topics you are addressing. Try this activity and see how powerfully engaging it really is.

MORPH GRID I: PRESENTATION AND FACILITATION

Captivate Strategy 11. Rhetorical Questions

Explanation (What is it!)

A rhetorical question encourages reflection within the listener. It is a nod at an idea with an implied question to the participant that "begs the question," but in an introspective manner. In other words, the listener is simply invited to think about the answer to the posed question but is not required to respond aloud. The rhetorical question itself, such as "Wouldn't we all like to have the highest test scores in the district?" is laid out there, with no expectation for an oral response. It is rhetorical, meaning it bounces back to the speaker, and a moment of silence is left behind for the listener to have an interior reflection—a thought not spoken to others but, rather, left hanging in the air for them to ponder at their leisure. Rhetorical questions are powerful tools used to invoke deep thinking about a profound idea. They can pepper a presentation with just the right amount of provocation to keep everyone mentally engaged.

Application (When to use it!)

Asking a rhetorical question can be used effectively in the midst of a talk to foster mindful engagement. The question might be asked at the beginning of the piece to set the stage for the answer the presenter is going to explore. This can provide an evocative backdrop to unfold some novel ideas. By asking the rhetorical question, minds are momentarily engaged in the target idea to be unraveled. "Isn't there a way we can do this so that all kids are successful?" is that kind of question. While this verbal volley is subtle and quiet, it still qualifies as an interactive strategy. It does serve to make the lecture more interactive with its softness. If it hooks the mind into a glimmer of a response, this rhetorical question has captivated the listener for that moment.

Elaboration (How to use it!)

For example, when a speaker asks, "How can we, as a country, accept a 30% illiteracy rate?" no formal answer is expected. Rather, it is a device used to assert or deny something. It asks the listener to dwell on the idea, even if only for a split second. In an effective use of this strategy, the rhetorical question might recur throughout the talk to punctuate the dilemma and sound the alarm in a repetitive fashion. "How can we, as a country, accept a 30% illiteracy rate?" is the question that reverberates in my mind. Do you see how this rhetorical question might take on a life of its own? Try this strategy and see how it might work for you.

MORPH GRID I: PRESENTATION AND FACILITATION

Captivate Strategy 12. Woven Questions

Explanation (What it is!)

A woven question is a question that is woven into the lecture itself by alluding to someone with a direct query. "John, do you agree with the author of the article when he states that, '*Data-directed instruction* is, perhaps, a more gentle term than *data-driven instruction*?'" This is called a woven question because it weaves into the fabric of the discussion with intention and direction. It is meant to engage an opinion and a response from the targeted person. By calling that person by name, there is a level of comfort and a rapport that is assumed by both the presenter and the participant. There is a high expectation implied that the person called upon to answer has an opinion and that he or she has the ability to form a cohesive response. The woven question, just as the rhetorical question, moves the typical one-way broadcast toward a more interactive lecture format.

Application (When to use it!)

Woven questions help make a lecture more interactive by involving the participants during the direct instruction or opening remarks. It turns the lecture, or *stand up model*, into a more robust two-way interactive discussion. Used in the heart of the talk, the woven question strategy creates a collegial atmosphere that warrants more conversation and more participation. It enlivens the session by involving participants in authentic ways. The woven questions can be sprinkled throughout the speech, creating a discussion-like format that is more inclusive than the standard speaker address.

Elaboration (How to use it!)

For example, in a classroom scenario, when the biology teacher is talking about DNA, he might ask, "Tim, do you agree or disagree with what Watson says?" (Watson and Crick are the geneticists who discovered the secret of DNA). This discussion technique is one that encourages reactions and responses from students. On the other hand, in a PD environment with adult learners, the question asked might be, "Michael, how would you explain the current practice of forming PLCs in our schools? How might you characterize this movement?" Again, this questioning strategy, directed to a specific person, can be an effective tool for fostering interactive environments in staff room sessions.

MORPH GRID I: PRESENTATION AND FACILITATION

Close Strategy 1. Circle Back to Beginning

Explanation (What it is!)

A memorable opening to a presentation can be anchored in the minds of the participants when the speaker circles back to that opening and ties it all together in the closing. The *Circle Back to Beginning* strategy creates a bookend effect, holding the ideas together—between the bookends, if you will. If you put the powerful opening image or funny cartoon back up on the screen after having used it to begin the session, the audience connects to what you said earlier. Circling back to the beginning with the opening music, a quote, or a joke is a natural way to bring about closure with an emotional connection.

Application (When to use it!)

Touch back on the opening quote, joke, or story. Circling back provides continuity and consistency to the presentation by emphasizing the theme, image, or quote in the two most important points in the talk—in the beginning and, again, in the end. These are the two times that leave the greatest impression in a presentation if they are used properly. However, the Circle Back to Beginning strategy is also effective when threaded through the presentation at intermittent points. When used in this way, the circle back strategy acts like a thread and ties ideas together throughout the presentation. The circle back concept is as old as time itself because it gives a beginning, middle, and an end to the piece. It is a natural format that puts a comfortable structure in place.

Elaboration (How to use it!)

For example, we use a cartoon called "Teaching Stripe to Whistle," and we talk about how it is not our job to just teach you to whistle but, rather, to ensure that you learn how to whistle. This makes that connection between teaching and learning. At the end of a presentation, we often ask, "If you have learned how to whistle, please let us hear you whistle."

In another example, we might circle back to an opening quote, a song, an image, a story, or even a key character that might have been referenced earlier. The Circle Back to Beginning strategy has so many applications; it is a strategy that can be used over and over again.

MORPH GRID I: PRESENTATION AND FACILITATION

Close Strategy 2. Key Points

Explanation (What it is!)

An agenda is a key strategy to announce the lineup for the session. It presents the main items to be addressed and gives the participants a big-picture view of things. A concise and clear agenda helps to clarify how all of the various points flow together. There are often people in the session who want an overview, a bird's eye view of the discussions and activities to follow. Just as we know that all learning is contextual, this agenda setting provides that backdrop to the day. People want a schema of the ideas so they can begin to make sense of things. In brief, the agenda is a highly traditional way to set that critical context for the session.

Application (When to use it!)

By summarizing critical learnings on a chart or in notes as the initial agenda of items to be addressed, the presenter provides a context for the material, as stated earlier. It also provides a nice touchback piece along the way because it is a quick glance summary that is easily revisited. It also works as an end-of-session summary. Returning to these bullet points at the end of a presentation is a sound presentation practice.

While the agenda is most often expected at the beginning of the session, it can also be a tool that unfolds as the session unfolds. In that way, you can add to the agenda as pertinent issues arise. Of course, this then becomes more of an organic agenda, a work in progress of sorts, but it can be a highly effective tool to stimulate interactivity and participant ownership, especially in smaller group settings.

Elaboration (How to use it!)

Most of the time, the key points are listed in the agenda as part of the PowerPoint or slide program. While that is a fairly effective way of getting the agenda out there, sometimes writing the key points on chart paper, versus simply listing them in a PowerPoint slide, emphasizes the critical information for participants. In this way, the presenter can make editorial comments as the agenda is revealed point-by-point.

Another idea that is used quite successfully by some is to create a beginning-of-the-session agenda with the participants. For example, sometimes we start a follow-up session with a chart that says, "What's Working, What's Not?" We then cluster the items on the list and assign priorities to the list, and that becomes the agenda for the day. It is powerful, of course, because it reflects the concerns of the group.

MORPH GRID I: PRESENTATION AND FACILITATION

Close Strategy 3. Take Away Item

Explanation (What it is!)

A *Take Away Item* is more than the handout, a notebook, a textbook, or any other resource that might be provided at the inservice. A Take Away Item, in this context, is something participants actually make as part of the workshop reflection piece to capture essentials from the presentation. It can be as simple as a homemade book of reminders, a foldable, or even a "Take Away Window" of ideas. Please note that the Take Away Item is not a gimmick or a fun little game; it is a transfer tool that makes the object perfectly and concretely clear to the learners, whether they are adults or children.

Application (When to use it!)

Even though these Take Away Items are created and utilized throughout the session, they are perfect tools to use as closure activities. Participants gather in groups of two, three, or four with their items and have a round-robin debriefing. Or the Take Away Item is designated to be used to share the information with others back onsite. It is small. It is portable, and it travels well, so it is appropriate as a transfer tool for onsite sharing.

Of course, the Take Away Item is also a viable strategy for teachers to use in their classrooms, with the same impact as a closure tool to a unit of study, a reading or viewing, or even a more robust activity such as a role play or simulation.

Elaboration (How to use it!)

For example, a Step Book or Flip Book on the six traits of writing becomes a resource for the teachers. They can use the same Step Book to help their students organize their writing, or they can use the Step Book idea to help students learn the six stages of metamorphosis.

The *Tiny Transfer Book,* named to remind teachers that all learning is for transfer, can be used to list all of the different strategies shared during the session. In turn, it can be used in the classroom with new material. This is a tiny little foldable that fits easily in your pocket or small ziplock jewelry baggie for field trips (you can add a small golf pencil). It makes a little clipboard when paper is clipped onto a small tile block. In addition, this tiny transfer book Take Away Item can be placed in a miniature cereal box, which can serve as a bookcase for several little books. The little book can also be taken away in an Animal Crackers box, which can create a little briefcase for the adult learners or the students.

MORPH GRID I: PRESENTATION AND FACILITATION

Close Strategy 4. Reflective Lead-In or Stem

Explanation (What it is!)

A reflective lead-in or stem statement is a prompt for further elaboration. It acts as a cueing device, a stimulus to spark further thinking. It can be used to cause the learner to think, plot, reflect, evaluate, or predict. Stem statements might look like this:

"A problem I'm having . . ."

"The hardest thing to do was . . ."

"A connection I made . . ."

"Next time . . ."

"If only I had . . ."

"One of my next steps is to . . ."

"I will use this when . . ."

Application (When to use it!)

Use a stem statement as a catalyst for higher-order thinking (analyzing, synthesizing, evaluating, hypothesizing, summarizing) after a strident input period. Give participants time to percolate with the ideas presented. Let their thoughts ferment, but give them a catalyst to get the process going.

By giving a reflective lead-in or stem statement, such as "I wonder . . ." or "My challenge is . . ." or "A conflicting idea . . . ," the participant is directed toward a reflective comment in the workshop setting. It helps to illuminate the target idea for deeper understanding.

Of course, these are also powerful techniques for stimulating reflection in the classroom. Classroom reflection is always warranted because the rapid pace of the interactions often does not allow time for the proper digestion and internalization of ideas. Here is a tool that works and is not terribly time consuming.

Elaboration (How to use it!)

For example, using the reflective lead-in, "Something that is confusing to me is . . ." when talking about the levels of transfer led to this statement by a participant: "Something that is confusing to me is the difference between *duplication* and *replication* in the levels of transfer."

Another stem-statement example overheard in a project-oriented workshop was, "I wonder if this topic is way too broad for a mini-presentation to my team? It seems overwhelming already."

MORPH GRID I: PRESENTATION AND FACILITATION

Close Strategy 5. Action Step

Explanation (What it is!)

An action step is a plan to take back to the classroom or staff room. The action step is set down with specific time-bound benchmarks. It is a commitment to do something as result of the new information. It becomes a delineation of what comes next in the ongoing learning of this concept. Action steps are the tools for sustained, job-embedded learning to occur in the professional learning setting. By creating several action steps, you are providing a concrete way for participants to connect what they are learning during an inservice to classroom practice.

Sometimes, these action steps might consist of a simple 1-2-3 list of things to do. Other times, they may have a priority of sorts attached to them: Things to Do Immediately, Things to Do Soon, Things to Do Down the Road! Yet all action steps, regardless of the format, are, indeed, a call to act!

Application (When to use it!)

Use action steps following any input that is to be applied. Facilitate the transfer and application of the ideas by delineating the few next steps. Remind participants of the action steps before they leave the site. Get them involved with these "what next" options to prepare them for onsite uses.

One other idea is to use action steps as shorthand for the process you are sharing, laying out the step-by-step process to be followed. "First, you. . . . Next, you. . . . And finally, you. . . ." This kind of scaffolding is not just for kids. It is also needed as an integral part of adult workshops and team meetings.

Elaboration (How to use it!)

Work out the action steps together or let teams or individuals set down their plan. For example, *"Tomorrow,* after taking roll, I will use thinking in pairs and have the students discuss what they might do to improve the lunch menu. I will do it again *after lunch* so that they become more familiar with the strategy. Then, the *next day,* I will use the Think Pair Share with a part of the homework assignment. *In one week,* I will be using the Think Pair Share to help them prepare to write. *In the future,* I can visualize using it for pre- and postreading interactions." Notice the sequence of her steps to application: tomorrow, after lunch, the next day, and so on.

MORPH GRID I: PRESENTATION AND FACILITATION

Close Strategy 6. Letter of Commitment

Explanation (What it is!)

The *Letter of Commitment* interaction usually requires a self-addressed, stamped envelope with a letter to one's self, to be mailed later by the leaders of the workshop. Participants are asked to write a letter to themselves, committing to use specific strategies in specific ways, in a specific timeframe. The letters are then delivered back to the teachers in a couple of weeks, so they can read, in their own hand, a letter to themselves about their commitment to integrate new ideas into their repertoire. The letter often appears as a surprise to the participants. They have forgotten all about it, so it has an emotional impact when it does arrive.

Application (When to use it!)

This is a particularly effective strategy when the professional learning opportunity has occurred during the summer holidays when school is not in session. It is easy to forget the dynamic ideas because of the time lapse between the staff room training and the classroom instruction. When that letter of commitment shows up, it truly is a powerful reminder of the experience, and it serves to jog memories about the prior session's work.

The Letter of Commitment is also a great way to spark thinking following a time lapse of several weeks. It appears, and again, it jogs the memory with personal notes to the teachers that hold a great deal of meaning because the promises are written in their own handwriting. Usually, there is a lot of laughter and high-energy conversation when the letters arrive, fueling good conversations around the anticipated applications.

Elaboration (How to use it!)

One example involves participants in literacy training. They wrote letters to themselves about using the seven strategies (schema, themes, questions, visualization, making inferences, summarizing, and metacognitive recovery strategies) that increase comprehension. When the letters arrived several months later, the teachers were able to revisit the strategies that they had learned earlier. The teachers talked about the ones they had tried immediately, and as they shared their applications, teachers came up with new ideas about how to use the strategies from these collegial conversations. They were also encouraged to use some of the strategies that they had not gotten to yet. In addition, the teachers continued their examination of the various strategies in terms of which ones were working well and what they needed to concentrate on in the future. In the end, they decided to divide the strategies into clusters for more emphasis.

Close Strategy 7. 3-2-1 Reflect

Explanation (What it is!)

This is a whole-class cooperative learning and reflection strategy that requires a look back at the session content. In this *3-2-1 Reflect* activity, all participants stand and engage in a discussion with others, preferably not at their table or with people with whom they have worked all day. In the first exchange, the two people talk about 3 things they *recall* from the day. Then they discuss 2 *insights* or connections that occurred during the day. Each participant, then, for the final interaction, discusses 1 *question* that is still lingering from the day's work.

Application (When to use it!)

Discussing the 3 recalls, 2 insights, and 1 question each person in the partnership has experienced naturally works well following the input of the day. It serves to end the workshop with energy and focus. Yet the 3-2-1 Reflect activity is also a dynamic "rebooting" strategy to begin the next session. It forces the participants to focus and remember the happenings from that previous session. It can also be used as an effective strategy for that after-lunch time, to consolidate the morning activities.

Elaboration (How to use it!)

As a specific example, following a day about multiple intelligences and differentiation strategies, one participant *recalled* three of the intelligences, made two *connections* between brain science and the need to differentiate (each brain is unique, and learning depends on background experiences), and finally, posed the question, "How will I be able to differentiate and, at the same time, deliver high standards for all?"

While the original 3-2-1 activity is used to capture recalls, insights, and questions, the 3-2-1 Reflect can be changed to a variety of prompts. For example, 3 new things you learned, 2 things that confirmed what you already knew, and 1 thing that you will do tomorrow. In sum, 3 learnings, 2 confirmations, and 1 application.

Yet another set of prompts might include 1 affirmation, 2 new twists on an old idea, and 3 new ideas. The participants can readily see the flexibility this strategy offers for reflective conversations. It is a strategy that can be used over and over again.

MORPH GRID I: PRESENTATION AND FACILITATION

Close Strategy 8. PMI—Plus! Minus! Interesting!

Explanation (What it is!)

PMI—Plus! Minus! Interesting! is derived from the work of Edward de Bono (1973). This evaluative strategy provides a wonderful tool for a facilitator to help participants see the pluses and minuses of an activity used in the session. It allows the participants to look at all sides of the issues and to evaluate what the positives were and what the negatives were. In turn, it affords them the opportunity to comment or reflect on aspects that were interesting, rather than just on the ones that seem to hold value as a plus or minus. In this way, the participants decontextualize the activity and begin to see it as a long-standing strategy that can be used over and over again.

Application (When to use it!)

The PMI strategy can be used to open a conversation about a topic, stirring up prior knowledge and attaching a value to it. In this way, participants get to review and renew their thinking on a particular subject before they begin to study it further. This works well with adult learners because they often bring so much prior information to the table.

Debriefing with PMI points is also a marvelously revealing way to end the session. It gives the participants a structured framework for analyzing and evaluating the day's activities and ideas. It is a highly reflective way to include all points of view, and it often reveals many facets of the topic under scrutiny.

Elaboration (How to use it!)

One example follows:

A PMI discussion was used to debrief the use of the concept of differentiating instruction in the classroom. A plus was that differentiation speaks to many learning styles in a classroom. A minus was the concern about how one teacher might create so many differentiated lessons. The interesting piece was the discovery that many teachers already are differentiating instruction.

Just a note: The last item, *Interesting*, might be changed to a *Delta (Change)* to indicate something one might change. It would then be PMD (Plus, Minus, Delta), and it would work in the same way as the PMI. Also, one can make a table like the one that follows to chart the comments.

Plus	Minus	Interesting

MORPH GRID I: PRESENTATION AND FACILITATION

Close Strategy 9. Analogy

Explanation (What it is!)

An analogy often compares something quite abstract to something that is more concrete. By discussing the likenesses of the more obscure abstraction to something more tangible, the learner can see the elements of each more clearly. In brief, using an analogy to compare the abstract to the concrete illuminates and clarifies the concept.

_____ (Concept) is like _____ (Concrete Object) because both _____.

To illustrate, professional learning that is sustained over time is compared to a compass: Sustained professional learning is like a compass because both have clearly visible directions.

Application (When to use it!)

At the end of the session, as a creative and interactive closing, participants focus on the idea at hand, such as "authentic assessments," and try to compare the idea to a concrete object or something tangible in order to understand the abstraction better. Taking turns, the participants might say:

"Authentic assessments are like a cornucopia of fruits that offer a variety of options."

"Authentic assessments are like a barometer because both are constantly measuring and assessing."

"Authentic assessments are like exercise workouts because both monitor progress."

Elaboration (How to use it!)

For example, a high-energy way to wrap up a workshop is with a whole-class cooperative structure, using the power of making an analogy. Have the class form a large circle. Each person, one at a time, on their own and without prompting, steps into the circle and gives an analogy that sums up what they have learned that day.

The presenter models a good analogy based on the topic that they have been teaching. For example, "Differentiated instruction is like a country buffet because both offer something for everyone." Or "Closing the achievement gap is like a long journey because both begin one step at a time."

The analogy can also be drawn as a visual metaphor or poster picture. By closing with an analogy, you help anchor the learning with creative thinking that is emotionally charged as each member rises to the occasion and offers his or her own analogy.

MORPH GRID I: PRESENTATION AND FACILITATION

Close Strategy 10. Yellow Brick Road

Explanation (What it is!)

Yellow Brick Road is the name of an interactive strategy in which members of the group are required to "take a stand," indicating their personal assessments on their own learning. It asks them to think about their level of understanding at a certain point in time and to indicate that level by selecting the appropriate corner of the room. The corners are labeled "Under Construction," "Rocky Road," "Yellow Brick Road," and "Highway to Heaven." Once participants are in their chosen corner, they discuss their self-assessments with a partner and explain why they have selected that particular label.

Application (When to use it!)

The Yellow Brick Road, like many of the ideas, can be used as an opening activity or as a closing activity. It is a whole-class cooperative structure, used to gauge how the group is feeling on a particular subject.

Designate four corners for the activity and have participants move to those corners to signal how well they understand the topic taught that day. Again, one corner of the room is "Road Under Construction," another corner is "Rocky Road," the third corner is "Yellow Brick Road," and the fourth corner is "Stairway to Heaven." After the participants move, have them discuss with the others in their corner why they felt like they belonged in that particular corner of the room.

Getting samples of some of the reasons given from each corner of the room models how, in high-achieving classrooms or staff rooms, it's not about what the teacher teaches, but what the students learn.

Elaboration (How to use it!)

For example, use the Yellow Brick Road activity to have participants reflect on their level of understanding about how to integrate the curricula following a PD on ten ways to integrate curricula. Some are excited and go directly to the "Stairway to Heaven" corner because they are already using robust models of curriculum integration, while others are more comfortable in the corner designated "Under Construction" because they are just beginning to integrate.

This is similar to the Human Graph strategy, but instead of a bar graph or line graph, it becomes more like a scatter graph. However, it is important to remember that it is the self-assessment and the ensuing discussion that the learners have that provide the insights.

MORPH GRID I: PRESENTATION AND FACILITATION

Close Strategy 11. Dial 4-1-1 for Information

Explanation (What it is!)

Dial 4-1-1 for Information is a reflection strategy for partner dialogue. This is similar to the 3-2-1 Reflect strategy, but it has a slightly different flavor. It asks for ideas, affirmations, and a call to action.

4 Ideas to take away

1 Affirmation of my work

1 Call to action for transfer

Everyone stands and finds a partner and then walks through the 4-1-1. Each partner shares 4 ideas, then each shares 1 thing that has been affirmed in the workshop, and finally, each partner commits to 1 call to action that will occur back at the school site.

Application (When to use it!)

This is an effective conversation to wrap things up, but as always, it can be used at the beginning of the next session to boost ideas from previous work because it has that rogue element of identifying an affirmation that was experienced. It is always nice to know that the work you're doing is on track and following best practices.

Elaboration (How to use it!)

Following a workshop on best instructional practices, one participant said this in her partnership dialogue:

4 Ideas

Four different ways to tap into the skill of finding similarities and differences: comparing and contrasting, classifying, using analogies, and using metaphors.

1 Affirmation

One thing that was affirmed was the need to activate prior knowledge to increase comprehension.

1 Call to Action

One thing I plan to do immediately is focus on telling students the *why* behind the many activities we do; sharing the why makes so much sense.

MORPH GRID I: PRESENTATION AND FACILITATION

Close Strategy 12. Aha! Oh, No!

Explanation (What it is!)

An *"Aha!"* moment or an *"Oh, no!"* moment are prompts for reflective dialogue about a viewing, a lecture input piece, or a reading. The idea is to think of one positive, or "aha," moment experienced during the input, and one negative or alarming moment that is the "Oh, no" moment. In this way, the participants are expected to think about all viewpoints, both good and bad, plus and minus, as they process the information.

The use of the "Aha!" and the "Oh, no!" emphasizes the personal aspect of participants' reactions and responses to the ideas under consideration. It allows the individuals to reflect in conjunction with their own beliefs and behaviors. These two statements also add a bit of drama to the conversation as each participant tries to make valid statements.

Application (When to use it!)

Use of these two stem statements fosters reflection among the participants, especially at the close of a session. It provides the platform for fruitful discussions. As the conversation unfolds about the "Aha" and "Oh, no" statements, both parties gain insights and make connections that help them deepen their understanding.

Using this during the session is another idea for appropriate application. It serves as a punctuation point to the input, allowing participants to digest the information and make sense of things. It's that pause in the session the refreshes participants as they take over the discussion format and share with each other.

Elaboration (How to use it!)

For example, "Turn to your partner and tell them two things about the session. Tell them one 'Aha!' statement and one 'Oh, no' statement that occurs to you."

An "Aha!" statement: "Aha! If it is true that the person doing the talking is the person doing the learning, then I have to orchestrate more interactions in my classroom."

"Oh, no!" statement: "Oh, no! If the home environment plays such a big role in early literacy, then we really have to work to get our parents involved with their kids in the literacy scene."

2

Morph Grid II

The Principal's Staff Meeting

Capture: Openers	Captivate: Middles	Close: Endings
1. Metaphors and Similes (page 45)	1. Fold-Over or Slip Slot Book (page 57)	1. Take Away Window (page 69)
2. Vignettes (page 46)	2. Pie Chart (page 58)	2. Mrs. Potter's Questions (page 70)
3. AB Pyramid Game (page 47)	3. Four-Fold Concept Development (page 59)	3. Reminder for Transfer (page 71)
4. Acronyms (page 48)	4. Debate Contrasting Statements (page 60)	4. Bookmark Think About (page 72)
5. Personality Profile (page 49)	5. List/Sort/Label (page 61)	5. Jingle (page 73)
6. Give One! Get One! (page 50)	6. Popcorn Out Ideas (page 62)	6. Shake and Break! I Appreciate! (page 74)
7. Accordion Book or Z Book (page 51)	7. Stack and Pack—I'll Be Back! (page 63)	7. Ms. Poindexter's Questions (page 75)
8. Mr. Parnes' Questions (page 52)	8. Probe! Pause! Paraphrase! or PACTS (page 64)	8. Art Journal (page 76)
9. Meet and Greet! Be Sweet! (page 53)	9. Create a Contest (page 65)	9. Prizes (page 77)
10. Costumes and Props (page 54)	10. PBL Scenarios (page 66)	10. Highlights! Insights! (page 78)
11. YouTube/Teacher Tube (page 55)	11. D & D/Drop and Debrief (page 67)	11. Staircase (page 79)
12. ABC Graffiti (page 56)	12. Photo Story (page 68)	12. Energizers (page 80)

INTRODUCTION

Principals are the ultimate instructional leaders in the building. They have a staff meeting every week. It is on the schedule. Whenever the instructional leaders of the building have an opportunity to have the faculty team in front of them, principals can and should take full advantage of that time. The staff meeting, in fact, provides the perfect platform to model active, engaging instructional strategies. As the principal or assistant principal conducts the business of the meeting, they can do it just as easily with an engaging strategy.

From Staff Room to Classroom II: The One-Minute Professional Development Planner is the perfect planning tool for principals who want to model the "lookfors" they want to see in the classroom walk-throughs. These leaders know the power of modeling the model.

DIRECTIONS

Roll a set of dice three times to select an activity for the three elements based on the numbers rolled. Be courageous and go with the actual numbers. Don't cheat. It will make your staff meetings lively, original, and effective.

1. *Capture* the PLC members' attention with openers.
2. *Captivate* with the "meat of the PLC session."
3. *Close* with keepers.

CATEGORICAL LISTING OF ALL MORPH TOOLS

Check Appendix A for an index of strategies by type of tool (e.g., collaborative tool or management tool).

CREATIVE OPTIONS

Remember, the strategies are interchangeable and often work as any of the three elements, depending on the context and how they are used. An opener may be used as a closer or even as part of the "meat" of the session. Be creative and use the grid of strategies with your own creative flair.

MORPH GRID II: STAFF MEETINGS

Capture Strategy 1. Metaphors and Similes

Explanation (What it is!)

Metaphors and similes are illuminating when working with a topic that is abstract or hard to define, such as formative assessments, differentiated learning, or integrated curriculum. They provide visual clues to the idea under scrutiny and help to make it clearer.

A *metaphor* is a visual comparison, such as "books are windows to the world," while a *simile* is a visual comparison expressed with the word *like* or *as.* For example, "Books are like windows to the world because they open the way to sights not seen before."

In either case, the metaphor or simile is a verbal tool that helps one visualize the abstract idea. Metaphors and similes paint pictures in our minds, making the ideas more real and more understandable.

Application (When to use it!)

Used as an opening piece, this activity helps make the concept concrete right at the start of the day. It can be used after the welcome and introduction to crystallize the concept at the very beginning of the session.

Have the whole group form a circle around the room so that everyone can see and hear each other. Have the facilitator say, "We are going to do a sharing of metaphors as a way to crystallize today's topic."

Elaboration (How to use it!)

"Differentiated instruction is like a three-ring circus because both have a lot going on, there are many things to hold your attention, and everyone can find something that interests them."

Another example: "Integrated curriculum is like a tapestry because both have patterns, threads running through them, and an ultimate design that shows through."

Instead of an open-ended metaphor, you might say, "We will compare the subject of the day to an animal." Using those instructions, you could say, "Differentiated instruction is like a chameleon because both are adaptable to their needs and talents."

MORPH GRID II: STAFF MEETINGS

Capture Strategy 2. Vignettes

Explanation (What it is!)

Vignettes are brief stories of people, in the form of tales or play scripts, that are used to make a brief telling point. Each vignette should demonstrate the key concept or idea that you are addressing. The vignettes represent a kind of story telling that gently or emphatically makes the point, depending on the nature of the tale you tell. A vignette in the form of a script has two teachers talking about literacy skills, making the point that "second chance readers" need explicit reading instruction so that as they *learn to read,* they will eventually be able to *read to learn.*

Application (When to use it!)

The use of a vignette is a powerful opening strategy because it is a friendly way to set the climate for a discussion. It usually captures the attention of the audience because everyone loves a story. As soon as you say, "I have a little tale to tell," you have their attention. They are poised and ready to hear the story, leaving you with a teach-able moment at hand.

Vignettes can also be appropriate to make a point, so they can also be used during the session. The best time to use them is either at some intersection of information or at the end, as an effective punctuation point to the session. As an editorial note on the use of vignettes, it is difficult to overuse this strategy. If the stories you have chosen have a clear and evident point, they can be used all day, every day—but a rambling story loses its luster very fast.

Elaboration (How to use it!)

In one example, in a presentation on the technology called *SMART Board,* the pre-senter did not actually have a working SMART Board. Instead, he showed PowerPoint slides of artifacts from three different teachers' applications, using an imaginary SMART Board. He described each application with a vignette or brief story, modeling the possi-ble use of the SMART Board. It worked! In fact, it was as if he had the SMART Board right in front of the participants the entire time. It was the stories that made the expe-rience believable and real.

Another example involves telling a story about data, and more important, the urgency of on-time data. A teacher tells the story of taking kids to the museum on a field trip. She talks about moving around the rooms and constantly counting heads to be sure that every student is accounted for, when she realizes three of them are missing. Immediately, she backtracks and gathers them up. She makes her point when she says, "I cannot wait until the end of the day to find the three students who got lost along the way. By then, it is too late. It is the same with achievement data. We need to find them early."

MORPH GRID II: STAFF MEETINGS

Capture Strategy 3. AB Pyramid Game

Explanation (What it is!)

The *AB Pyramid Game* is like the old Password game or the new Pyramid game, in which one participant gives word clues to a partner. The partner is supposed to find the target word from the clues given. AB partners sit, with the A partner facing the screen and the B partner facing away from the screen. A category for the words is named and then words are given on the screen. The A partner reads the words silently and then begins to give clues to the B partner, in order to elicit a response. Once the B partner responds, the A partner can give another clue. As the B partner gets the words correct, the A partner moves on to the next word. It is high energy, and uproariously funny at times, as the partners collaborate to find the words and finish the game as winners!

Application (When to use it!)

The AB Pyramid Game offers an opportunity for the staff members to get on the same page by involving them in an interactive game that highlights words related to the topic at hand. It also serves as a great mixer because it gets the teams on board and builds team spirit. The AB Pyramid Game is a nice way to begin a session with a bang!

However, the game also works well right after a lunch break, when participants become a bit lethargic. The energy really surges once the game is under way. It also offers a perfect opportunity to move participants into new groups and partnerships, which always energizes the room.

It is also a powerful ending strategy because it is a great way to review key vocabulary words and concepts that were utilized throughout the session. It keeps the participants on task as the day winds down, and it also provides an enthusiastic end to the session.

Elaboration (How to use it!)

"Generation Savvy" is a current topic for school leadership. Put six words on the screen or chart and ask the A partners to give clues and cues to the B partners, using six words that illuminate "Generation Savvy." These words can include, for example, *Millennials, Gen Xers, Traditionals, Generation Y, Baby Boomers*, and *Nexters*. Once the B partners say the word on the chart, the A partners should move to the next word and give new clues and cues for that word, until they have gone through all six words. Then have the partners change seats, and have the B partner give clues and cues for the next list of six words around the same topic. Additional "Generation Savvy" words could include *Seasoned-Staff, Newbies, Veterans, Old Timers, New Teachers*, and *Start-Ups*. This is a high-energy and highly engaging way to get everyone on board.

MORPH GRID II: STAFF MEETINGS

Capture Strategy 4. Acronyms

Explanation (What it is!)

An acronym is a quick summary of key bullet points that uses the letters of the word to create an advanced organizer. The completed acronym helps the participants grasp the nugget of what you are teaching. For example, a good set of subskills for active, attentive listening is summarized by the acronym PACTS.

P   Paraphrase (Rephrase in your own words)
A   Affirm (Give positive feedback: a nod, uh huh, agreed!)
C   Clarify questions (Ask for details, an example, a restatement)
T   Test options (Give further prompts, "Would you say . . . ?")
S   Sense tone (Make inferences and notice nuances)

PACTS becomes a quick guide, or a reminder of specific behaviors, that helps one exhibit strong listening skills. It provides a way to think about listening skills more explicitly.

Application (When to use it!)

Acronyms are useful throughout the duration of a workshop, but if, and when, the acronym is introduced early in the session, it becomes a powerful pivot point for further work. It is the touchback point throughout the day, providing an anchor to the key points.

An acronym is a memory peg that has been used successfully in classroom situations and in staff rooms. Acronyms are used as magnets. Many subsequent ideas can be attached to the magnet so that, at the end of the day, the key ideas can be remembered more readily.

Elaboration (How to use it!)

To use acronyms effectively, use the letters of the key concept, such as A-S-S-E-S-S-M-E-N-T, to have participants unpack the ideas embedded in it. This can be used as a partner task or a small team task, and it generates a lot of creative interaction.

A   All day long
S   Summative
S   Student-centered
E   Every day
S   Standards-based
S   Sensible
M   Measurement
E   Evaluative
N   Noted observations
T   Teachable moment

The brainstorm and conversation help to unpack the idea quite comprehensively. Try it in several settings, with several topics, and see how it works for you.

MORPH GRID II: STAFF MEETINGS

Capture Strategy 5. Personality Profile

Explanation (What it is!)

The *Personality Profile* is an amusing game that can be used to build teamwork through disclosure of what each person's drawing of a pig might look like. It is a pseudopsychological profile, used for humor and fun. Here is how it goes: Ask participants to draw their version of a pig; then, use the personality profile analysis that follows to "unpack the personalities" and have some fun.

Personality Profile

Directions: Draw a pig!

Analysis:

- Top of page—optimist
  Middle of page—realistic
  Bottom of page—pessimist

- Facing straight—direct, likes to play Devil's advocate, doesn't avoid issues
  Facing left—traditional, friendly, remembers birthdays and dates
  Facing right—innovative, action-oriented, not family oriented

- Very detailed—analytical, cautious, suspicious
  Little detail—emotional, bored with detail, naive, risk taker

- Four feet—secure, stubborn, has firm beliefs
  Fewer than four feet—insecure, going through major life changes

- Larger the ears, the better listener a person is
  Larger the head, the bigger the person's ego
  Longer the tail, the better the person's memory

Share and compare as teams. Do not take it too seriously, but let it provide a format for talking about the following idea: "The more diverse a team, the richer the product."

Application (When to use it!)

The Personality Profile is a way to get the staff talking and interacting at the beginning of the year or term. It is fun, but it is also a great way to introduce the concept of differences in staff and differences in students. Have teachers respond to the questions independently, and then, as the leader, read the analyses. Also use this strategy as a high-energy activity in the midst of a long, comprehensive session that seems to need a little lightening up.

Elaboration (How to use it!)

The preceding notes explain how one might use this idea. It also works well with students.

MORPH GRID II: STAFF MEETINGS

Capture Strategy 6. Give One! Get One!

Explanation (What it is!)

Give One! Get One! is a strategy that gets the group up and moving. Each person is given a piece of paper with a set of leading statements on it that require responses from others. One person approaches another person and gives a response to one of the written statements. In turn, the giver gets one from the partner. Give One! Get One! describes the process, as the people continue to go on to the next person. This keeps the interaction moving along and simultaneously works as a way of introducing the topic under discussion. It helps the group members stir up prior knowledge about the agenda item. See the examples that follow.

Application (When to use it!)

As an opener, a great way to get the interactions started is to pose a set of questions about an upcoming event or issue. It could be about parent conferences, report cards, state tests, the teacher evaluation plan, or any number of issues that come up and appear on the staff meeting agenda. By giving each person a copy and having the staff walk around the room giving and getting answers, the strategy acts as an icebreaker. It gets things going on a positive note and eases the way into the topic at hand. Using this interactive strategy does not have to take a lot of time. It can work in a ten-minute slot, yet it does afford an opportunity to get a few things out about the topic up for discussion. Do not forget, it is a viable way to begin a session, but also to end a meeting!

Elaboration (How to use it!)

Use the Give One! Get One! strategy to invite meaningful interaction among staff members. For example, prepare a set of statements that focus on a particular topic, and ask the staff to move about the room, talking to others, as they give one and get one.

Topic: Parent Conferences

1. Some parents are uncomfortable coming to parent conferences because . . .

2. When students leave a note on their desk to the parent, it. . . .

3. Who should do the most talking at the parent conference?

4. The goal of parent conferences is . . .

5. Agree or disagree: Students should come to parent conferences.

6. A benefit of conferences with parents is . . .

7. My most successful strategy for parent conferences is . . .

8. One way to involve the parents more in parent conferences might be to . . .

MORPH GRID II: STAFF MEETINGS

Capture Strategy 7. Accordion Book or Z Book

Explanation (What it is!)

The *Accordion Book* is a foldable that is folded back and forth until it looks like an accordion, or a *Z*. The advantage of this foldable is that both sides of the page are available for use. Of course, you can change the size of the book page by changing the size of the paper strip. Once you know what you need, cut or tear the paper into strips of the correct size and then proceed to fold the strip back and forth, back and forth, until it looks like an accordion. Make a cover title and then set up the pages as an advanced organizer.

Application (When to use it!)

This tool is appropriate for note taking and for summarizing key points to take away from the staff meeting or the team session. There is nothing as valuable as a succinct set of notes for a later review of the salient points. While traditional note-taking works, it is helpful to have a separate tool that captures all the information in one place.

Of course, the real value behind this strategy is that it models a technique for note taking and a tool for summarizing that teachers can immediately take back to the classroom. Whenever the leader has the chance to demonstrate an engaging instructional strategy, in the end, the students are the winners. Setting a good example is not only the best way to influence someone, it is the only way.

Elaboration (How to use it!)

The Accordion Book can be used for the eight multiple intelligences identified for differentiation. On each page, write one of the multiple intelligences and then add a symbol to reflect its essence. In turn, add various classroom activities that epitomize the intelligence:

Visual/Spatial Intelligence	
Symbols, graphics, drawings, DVDs, YouTube, sketches, graphic organizers, art, graphic arts software, picture books, cartoons, comics, political cartoons, illustrations, mental memory techniques . . .	

MORPH GRID II: STAFF MEETINGS

Capture Strategy 8. Mr. Parnes' Questions

Explanation (What it is!)

Discussed by Sidney Parnes as a way to take learning to new levels of meaning, *Mr. Parnes' Questions* ask two simple things:

1. How does this connect to something you already know?

2. How might you use this in the future?

When Parnes says that these two questions take learning to a new level, he is referring to the metacognitive nature of these questions. They take one full circle, from the cognitive information and typical answers to the metacogntive. These are the kinds of questions that require reflection in order to respond fully. In fact, these kinds of metacognitive questions move us beyond the cognitive and into that reflective realm of connections and applications. When one is asked to make connections and push application, that person is processing the information in personally relevant ways. In fact, that person is building *schema*, or connections and patterns that are meaningful only to that individual.

Application (When to use it!)

Mr. Parnes' Questions can be used anytime, but they are often extremely effective early in the session or meeting, when introducing ideas that you want the group to own. By asking participants how the concepts connect, you force them to tap into their prior knowledge and make personal meaning of the ideas. When you ask the participants how they might use this in the future, you are pushing transfer and moving them to relevant applications. Mr. Parnes' Questions have the power to transform mundane information into purposeful and actionable learning. These questions truly do lift the learning to new levels because the learner must connect and apply.

Elaboration (How to use it!)

Examples of Mr. Parnes' Questions apply to many staff meeting topics and issues. Discussions about new report cards, changes in disciplinary actions, or emerging data on student performance are typical meeting agenda items that might work well with Mr. Parnes' Questions.

Whatever the topic under study, these two questions direct the staff members to make relevant connections and useful applications right on the spot. With that kind of transfer, and due to its personal relevance, they will really remember the discussion. Of course, it is also a great model for teachers to use in the classroom. Modeling these questions in the meeting will, hopefully, encourage classroom application.

MORPH GRID II: STAFF MEETINGS

Capture Strategy 9. Meet and Greet! Be Sweet!

Explanation (What it is!)

As a way to model collaboration and conversation, ask the staff members to meet and greet their tablemates. Ask them to say, "Good morning" (or "Good afternoon"), and *mean it!* Tell them to make sure they know everyone at their table because they will be working together as a team. This may not be necessary in a faculty meeting, but it might be useful early in the year or whenever cross-departmental teams are working together because they may not know everyone in the various departments, especially in large high schools.

Once they have performed the social function of introductions, you might ask them to share some point that addresses the issue of the day. It acts as a warm up to the issue at hand and stirs up prior knowledge about that topic. While this is a simple strategy, it models the social aspect of collaborative work. It makes a point about how to meet and greet others on the team or on the committee. It is also simply good manners and proper etiquette.

Application (When to use it!)

The *Meet and Greet! Be Sweet!* strategy may be used whenever—and every time—you want the members to change partners to freshen up the interaction. Sometimes, changing up the pairs or trios changes the entire conversation. The new dynamics may change the tenor of the conversation as people offer opinions and ideas. In turn, by changing partners and setting up the meet and greet, and as people are becoming more comfortable with the new people, their opinions are often offered in a tempered manner, with more respect for the new points of view. In some cases, the content actually changes as differing perspectives are put on the table and explored together.

Elaboration (How to use it!)

For example, you might say, "Meet and greet and . . ."

" . . . share a differentiation strategy that works for you."

" . . . talk about a concern you have from the data."

" . . . compare your 'no-fail, best practice' that works every time."

" . . . share one thing you do for parent conferences that parents love."

MORPH GRID II: STAFF MEETINGS

Capture Strategy 10. Costumes and Props

Explanation (What it is!)

One of the most visible and obvious ways to capture the attention of the teachers as they arrive for a staff meeting is for the principal or leader to enter the room in a costume of sorts. It sounds pretty hokey, but even a hat or a noticeable prop of some kind will do the trick. It really creates energy in the room as the group has a hearty laugh at the principal's or leader's expense. Yet wearing a symbolic baseball cap (to cap off the year), or an umpire's vest (to revisit the school rules that students must adhere to), or holding an umbrella (to think about an umbrella theme for the month) raises the curiosity of staff members as they wonder what in the world the gimmick is and what is about to occur. It is a simple, funny, fun, and effective strategy.

Application (When to use it!)

The costumes and props can be used at any time to make a telling point. They help the leader to introduce an idea, to emphasize an issue, to summarize long-term initiatives, or to simply talk about a recurring situation. The key to knowing when it is best used depends on who it is, what he or she hopes to accomplish, and how confident she or he feels about playing this silly kind of role-play game.

However, if one is ready, willing, and able to pull it off, the use of costumes, hats, props, and so on is a dramatic tool for the traditional staff room meeting and, more often than not, can have a huge impact. It becomes one of those incidents that are talked about in the teacher's lounge for a very long time to come.

Elaboration (How to use it!)

One memorable example involves a principal who had adhesive lint removers on every table at a staffroom meeting as a symbol of the new guidelines for school safety that must "stick" in the minds of the students. Another wore a baseball cap to illustrate the team spirit needed in the newly formed professional learning communities (PLCs).

Still another brave soul donned a frilly, over the neck, wraparound apron to introduce his new initiative on brain-healthy, brain-friendly foods. The health and wellness campaign for students, mandated by the state for all schools, called for immediate action in the district. This ploy worked quite well for this particular building principal. It got everyone's attention, bar none, and it made a real impact on the importance of the initiative.

MORPH GRID II: STAFF MEETINGS

Capture Strategy 11. YouTube/Teacher Tube

Explanation (What it is!)

YouTube videos (found at www.youtube.com) are short, funny, and to the point. Teacher Tube videos are short, funny, and to the point...about teaching issues. There are a number of clips, as brief as one to three minutes, that can be used to set the scene for the topic of the moment. Great meeting starters, YouTube/Teacher Tube videos are so entertaining that they can be viewed and reviewed a number of times. Here are some commonly used titles you can search for on the Internet that are sure to work to introduce your meeting topic:

Shift Happens

Cowboys Herding Cats

Airplanes

Running With the Squirrels

Cheering Helps

How to Read a Book

Escalator

PowerPoint Tips

The Office: How to Make a Presentation

Application (When to use it!)

The use of the YouTube/Teacher Tube videos as meeting starters is an appropriate and effective use of this strategy. It gets everyone's attention and immediately sets the stage for a lively discussion. The fact that these clips are so short and usually so funny makes them great energizers for staff, especially if the meeting is after school when everyone is feeling fatigue from a busy day.

Also, using YouTube/Teacher Tube in the middle of the session offers a nice interlude or relief to the discussion or debate that is being pursued. It brings a humorous moment to the scene and, at the same time, provides a catalyst for further conversation.

Elaboration (How to use it!)

One example of using YouTube as a starter is with the clip titled "Reading a Book." It is about the hesitancy some staff members reveal as meaningful change comes into the school setting. The people in the video are unsure and timid about using this "new-fangled instrument" called the book. The story harkens back to the same feelings many had as they were, or are, trying to master new technologies. Yet it is a gentle reminder that when change happens, it eventually does become the norm.

MORPH GRID II: STAFF MEETINGS

Capture Strategy 12. ABC Graffiti

Explanation (What it is!)

ABC Graffiti is an advanced organizer that uses the alphabet as the format for brainstorming words, phrases, synonyms, and ideas to unpack a focus word or concept. Working in pairs or teams, large poster paper is set up with the target word at the top and the letters of the alphabet displayed in two columns. Using *response in turn,* the team brainstorms as many words as possible, placing each word by the matching letter of the alphabet. Teams learn quickly that they should not list them in alphabetical order, but rather should say the words randomly and then place the words on the paper in the order that they are called.

Application (When to use it!)

The applications for this strategy are unending. The advanced organizer provides the perfect platform for generating a lot of vocabulary words around a specific target concept at the start of the meeting. It stirs up prior knowledge and starts the thinking about the topic of the day. It can also be a teambuilding exercise when used at the beginning of the meeting because teams become somewhat competitive, trying to complete the list with the needed 26 words. In fact, it really becomes lots of fun as teams try to complete the task. They even start stealing words from other groups to finish their list. This makes a marvelous modeling of interactive, engaged learning that teachers can use immediately in their classroom lessons.

Elaboration (How to use it!)

The ABC Graffiti strategy is great to unpack common vocabulary words and concepts.

Staff Room Topics

Literacy	Formative assessment
Comprehension	Mental math
Differentiation	Parent conferences
Data	Report cards

Classroom Topics

Energy	Algebra
Civil war	Fiction
Genre	Photosynthesis
Equal	Symmetry
Supply and demand	Tragedy

MORPH GRID II: STAFF MEETINGS

Captivate Strategy 1. Fold-Over or Slip Slot Book

Explanation (What it is!)

The *Fold-Over* or *Slip Slot Book* is a foldable that can be used for note taking during the meeting. It can be made from one piece of paper or more, depending on the desired number of pages. To create a Fold-Over Book, simply fold the papers in half the short way (hamburger bun style), not the long way (like a hot dog bun). This fold over is the easiest little book to make.

However, if the preference is for the Slip Slot Book, you need at least two sheets of paper that are the same size. Fold one in half with the hamburger bun fold. Then, tear a slot in the middle section of the fold to create a thin opening about an inch short of the top and bottom. Next, take the other sheet, fold it in half the same way, and make an inch tear at the top and the bottom. Slide this in through the slot in the first page. The inside page is now held secure and is ready for note taking. This takes a little more effort to make, but is held together more securely by the inserted page.

Application (When to use it!)

These simple foldables provide viable models of note-taking tools for students of all ages. By actually using it in the staff meeting, teachers experience the ease of use and value of these kinds of active learning tactics. Try using one in the heart of the meeting, as the discussion gets into full swing. Have the teachers make the book with some key words or magnet words at the top of the page. Then have them reference the various pages as a point of concern becomes the focus of the discussion. This simple tool provides a designated place to take down key notes for later review or for the next meeting.

Elaboration (How to use it!)

An example of the Fold-Over Book or the Slip Slot Book model, made from two pieces of paper, involves the principal as she is setting the stage for developing PLCs with the staff. The booklet might have the following formatting.

Cover: Professional Learning Communities

1. Defining a PLC

2. The PLC Mission

3. The PLC Vision

4. PLC Protocols

5. PLC Expectations

6. PLC Requirements

As the meeting discussion unfolds, the teachers can capture the critical information on the pages of the foldable. It will be a handy guide for the first PLC meeting the teams hold.

MORPH GRID II: STAFF MEETINGS

Captivate Strategy 2. Pie Chart

Explanation (What it is!)

The *Pie Chart* is a graphic depiction of information that is easy to reference in a discussion. It allows each staff member to chart information specific to the class and can also be used building-wide to graph grade level, department, or schoolwide data. Once they have made the Pie Chart template, have teachers chart their responses. For example, one principal, who was focusing on engaged learning time, asked his staff members to chart the four elements of how they use one class period. He asked them to chart these four activities:

- Teacher talk
- Student talk
- Student hands-on activity
- Checking for understanding

Application (When to use it!)

This graphing activity makes a wonderful pivot point for articulation across grade levels, PLCs, and departmental and vertical teams. It is a visible depiction of the information that is under discussion and thus provides a viable tool to compare and contrast data. Using this as part of the meeting agenda is a powerful way to get staff members intensely involved in the conversation. Everyone likes to have real, authentic, relevant data to cite and analyze. There is nothing as compelling as that for a meaningful and significant discussion because the teacher already has a stake in it with the graphed data.

This could also be used at the very beginning of the meeting, as a starting point, with the data graphed and ready to read and discuss. Of course, it might also be used as a closing piece for consideration or data gathering before the next meeting. Again, it is a staff room tool for the principal to model that easily becomes a classroom tool for teachers.

Elaboration (How to use it!)

One other example of the Pie Chart strategy is to ask teachers to chart on a pie graph the kinds of data they use most frequently:

- Standardized tests
- Daily work
- Weekly quizzes
- Chapter tests
- Unit tests
- End of term tests
- End of course tests

Captivate Strategy 3. Four-Fold Concept Development

Explanation (What it is!)

The *Four-Fold Concept Development* is a differentiation tool that is used to understand a concept or idea. In teams, the poster paper is folded into four corner sections. Then, it is folded again by holding the folded edges and making a small triangle fold. When opened, this triangle fold will appear as a diamond shape for the focus word. Once opened, the teachers should label the sections according to the diagram below. From that, they should develop a focus word by moving from one section to the next in this order: list, rank, compare, illustrate.

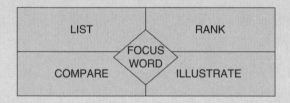

1. To *list*, the teachers brainstorm synonyms or ideas for the focus word.

2. To *rank*, they look over the list and determine the top three words.

3. To *compare*, they use the following sentence: "_____ (focus word) is like _____ (concrete object), because both are 1 _____, 2 _____, 3 _____." (They give three comparisons.)

4. To *illustrate*, they draw a visual metaphor or picture of the object being compared.

Application (When to use it!)

Use the Four-Fold Concept Development template activity to unpack an idea or issue that is the focus of the staff meeting. This allows for plenty of teamwork and high-energy interactions that really get to the heart of the matter with the multimodal activities. Use this strategy in a staff meeting to get teams to examine the idea of new report cards, a discipline plan, parent conferences, integrated technology, new SMART Boards, or anything that is on the agenda for discussion and exploration. This is a no-fail strategy that principals can use to model engaged learning instructional strategies.

Elaboration (How to use it!)

Examples of focus words include many of the same words that are interwoven into building-level concerns that may be instructional (differentiation, assessment for learning, performance tasks), behavioral (referrals, character development, values), or related to the building (graffiti, teacher duties, parents). Whatever the topic, it is an easy way to get the teachers onboard and participating. In turn, they will take this back to their classroom and use it with their students.

MORPH GRID II: STAFF MEETINGS

Captivate Strategy 4. Debate Contrasting Statements

Explanation (What it is!)

The idea to *Debate Contrasting Statements* is a platform for constructive controversy. Debate is a healthy, stimulating, and illuminating solution to issues that are often confusing and ambiguous. The use of contrasting statements gives everyone a chance to debate the issues.

Instruction is assessment! Assessment is instruction!

While not entirely contrasting statements in the literal sense, these two statements open the door for a range of opinions. Some will say, "Yes, good instruction inherently has an assessment aspect to it because teachers check for understanding, and assessment inherently has an instructive element because teachers use the assessments to drive instructional decisions."

Others might say, "Instruction is not assessment. They are not the same thing; they are separate and distinct in the classroom. Thus, it follows that assessment is not instruction. Assessment is about judgment, while instruction is about teaching and learning."

Application (When to use it!)

Debating contrasting statements is a powerful strategy that can be used to uncover all the facets of an issue during the heart of the meeting. It is a highly interactive activity that beckons all participants to weigh in on the complexities. It often creates quite a divisive factor, which calls for clarity from both sides.

At its best, debating truly sheds light on the many facets of complex ideas. As people articulate their stances on the debate, many interesting facts are uncovered. Of course, it takes a skillful mediator to handle the different sides of the argument. At the end of the day, however, a lively discussion is always a good way to unpack diverse opinions.

Elaboration (How to use it!)

Example 1

"If you're talking, you ain't learning," versus "The person doing the talking is the person doing the learning."

Example 2

"The most expensive staff development is the one teachers don't transfer into the classroom," versus "The only thing worse than training teachers who leave is not training teachers, and having them stay."

Captivate Strategy 5. List/Sort/Label

Explanation (What it is!)

This strategy is a variation on the traditional brainstorm. Instead of simply generating a list of ideas, this calls for two subsequent steps: (1) sort the list and then (2) label the resulting categories. The power of this strategy is that it requires both creative thinking in the brainstorm and critical thinking in the sorting and labeling. In fact, the inductive model of instruction enhances the higher-order thinking required in this activity. *Inductive* means that specifics are used to determine the general ideas. Thus, the specifics are labeled and then re-sorted into big-idea categories. It is an analysis-synthesis tool that helps one to think through both the specifics and the generalizations of an idea.

One example is to have staff members brainstorm technology skills their students need. Then, have them sort the list into groups (narratives, spreadsheets, slides, graphs, objects, etc.) and label each of the groups (e.g., Word, Excel, Cad/Cam).

Application (When to use it!)

Use this strategy to unpack a key topic or idea that is the focus of the discussion. Model how this activity fosters vocabulary building, classification, and generalization skills that are part and parcel of the higher-order thinking classroom.

Elaboration (How to use it!)

Another example works well when the staff is working in teams. Brainstorm words for *differentiation* (simpler reading, cooperative buddy, performance options, hands-on learning, visual products, translation partner, and assessment choices); sort the words that were brainstormed (simpler reading-content; cooperative buddy-process; hands-on learning-process, etc.); then, the final step is to label the groupings (e.g., cooperative buddies and hands-on learning are grouped as "multimodal processes").

DIFFERENTIATION		
List Differentiation Ideas	*Sort Into Like Groups*	*Label the Groups*
Simpler reading	Simpler reading	Differentiate the content
Cooperative buddy	Cooperative buddy Translation partner	Differentiate the process
Hands-on learning		

MORPH GRID II: STAFF MEETINGS

Captivate Strategy 6. Popcorn Out Ideas

Explanation (What it is!)

This is a participation strategy that allows teachers to *pop up* with an idea, similar to the way popcorn starts popping slowly and then popcorns out rapidly as the kernels start popping faster and faster. The same phenomenon occurs as people start popping up with ideas and then others piggyback on the ideas until they are popping fast and furiously. It fosters spontaneity and creative thinking. This is simply a strategy to get people to join in, informally, as ideas occur to them. It is a quick way to get the staff involved in sharing their opinions and often creates a flurry of ideas. It may begin with participation from those who are confident in their thinking, but if allowed enough wait time, others will follow.

Application (When to use it!)

After participants are asked to either turn to a partner and share or share ideas as a table team, instead of calling on tables or asking for a show of hands, the presenter says, "Just let your ideas popcorn up." This strategy gives permission to the group to be spontaneous and vocal. It energizes the sharing as tables begin to "popcorn" their ideas, and other tables listen and then popcorn their own.

It can also be used as a brainstorming technique, as the leaders generate a long list of ideas that begin a session. This still may occur in the heart of the meeting, but the team-generated list creates a bank of homespun ideas to work with. It also follows that this popping can be used toward the end of a discussion to summarize key points, as people "popcorn out" with key points to take away.

Elaboration (How to use it!)

One way to use this strategy is to ask for teachers to popcorn out as they think of concerns they have in terms of discipline in the common areas (lunch room, hallways, auditorium, playground). This begins a conversation on the schoolwide discipline plan, which is the topic under consideration for the meeting.

Another idea is to use the popcorn out idea in a discussion about parent conferences. Ask for ideas about how various teachers get parents actively involved in the conference. What do they do to make parents comfortable enough to join the discussion? As ideas popcorn out, others get the benefit of hearing new ways of working with the parents. It has a natural flow to it once the "popping" starts in the meeting.

MORPH GRID II: STAFF MEETINGS

Captivate Strategy 7. Stack and Pack—I'll Be Back!

Explanation (What it is!)

Stack and Pack—I'll Be Back is a management tool. It simply helps teams organize their materials on the table so others might use that spot for a work task. Stack and Pack is used when the principal wants to move staff members to work with another partner or group. This is done, even in an hour-long meeting, to change the dynamics of the groups or teams. Stack and Pack is a strategy that makes it clear that there is going to be a shift of activities. It acts like an exclamation point in the course of the meeting, causing everyone to sit up and take notice.

Application (When to use it!)

To energize the meeting, about halfway through, or just before a new section or activity, have the teachers "stack and pack" their papers and other stuff and move to a new spot. In this way, they are ready to work with a new partner or group, which always puts a new spin on things. Then, they will return to their original spot at the table with their stuff.

While most people do not really want to move during a meeting or session, the energy that is created by changing groups or teammates is well worth the initial reluctance to get up and change seats. Trust the process and follow through with a Stack and Pack tactic. Then, be aware of the new energy and refreshed dynamics in the room.

Elaboration (How to use it!)

One example of a strategic Stack and Pack—I'll Be Back move was modeled during a staff meeting that was focused on talking about PLCs and their work in the school. It was understood that some PLCs were working well, making lots of meaningful decisions about data-based instructional changes, while other PLCs were in a kind of limbo. These latter PLCs were meeting, but did not have a feeling of being purposeful or successful.

To facilitate the conversation among the team members of the various PLCs, the principal called for a Stack and Pack and asked people to move to groups that included members from at least three different PLCs. The ensuing discussions were enhanced by the mix of the teams. The staff was able to share things that were working and things that were not, in confidential, collegial groups. It created a safe climate to talk about some of the topics that might have been awkward to say aloud to the large group.

MORPH GRID II: STAFF MEETINGS

Captivate Strategy 8. Probe! Pause! Paraphrase! or PACTS

Explanation (What it is!)

Probe! Pause! Paraphrase! is a powerful dialogue strategy that focuses on intent listening. As one partner shares, the other partner responds with three distinct tactics that serve to enhance the discussion with what is often called *attentive*, or active, listening.

Probe—Clarify with questions for understanding

Pause—Take time to find connections in your mind

Paraphrase—Use your own words to restate

PACTS is another active, attentive listening strategy that calls for the listener to do the following:

Paraphrase—"In other words. . . ."

Affirm—"I agree. . . ."

Clarify—"Do you mean . . . ?"

Test options—"Is it similar to . . . ?"

Sense tone—"Are you feeling frustrated?"

Application (When to use it!)

The use of these dialogue and listening strategies is most helpful during the discussion that ensues after all participants have introduced a topic for scrutiny. Simply by pairing the teachers up and directing the dialogue with either three Ps or PACTS, principals or leaders facilitate robust conversations among the staff.

While these are listening strategies that can be used in many situations, by modeling and practicing these tactics in a staff meeting, the principal is setting the stage for them to be transferred into various situations in the classroom.

Elaboration (How to use it!)

One grand example of the three Ps and PACTS was when a principal used the strategy after talking about the focus on higher-order thinking skills during class discussions. As teachers practiced the PACTS and the three Ps, they literally experienced the power of this concept. They were engaged in higher-order thinking as they strived to respond and elaborate as the listening partner probed, paused, and paraphrased. The strategies have so many uses to increase the richness of discussions in the staff room and in the classroom. Once students get used to them, they will naturally incorporate them into their repertoire of active listening behaviors.

MORPH GRID II: STAFF MEETINGS

Captivate Strategy 9. Create a Contest

Explanation (What it is!)

Create a Contest is a strategy that gets people excited about an idea by turning it into a competitive situation. The contest can be framed for individuals or for teams competing against each other. The contest can be a small part of the interaction or it can be the main attraction. Yet the contest must be structured carefully if its purpose is to be clearly understood and skillfully executed. In the end, the contest should create an energy that can be directed toward the topic under discussion. It might be a race to brainstorm the most ideas within a given time frame; it might be a relay, in which team members take turns trying to complete a task before the other team can; or the contest might be a team effort, such as creating a mural or slogan that depicts the idea under consideration.

Application (When to use it!)

There is nothing like a little contest to get the competitive spirit to kick in. This is a great strategy to captivate the group in the middle of the meeting, when things might be bogging down. Contests really do heat up the room with excitement, so whenever it seems appropriate to energize the situation, you might want to use the contest idea.

Contests mean one group is trying hard to beat another group. Healthy competition helps build teamwork skills and facilitates real bonding. Everyone seems to get into the spirit quite naturally as the contest itself unfolds. It's the nature of the beast, so to speak.

Elaboration (How to use it!)

For example, toward the end of a meeting on types of communication used by all (formal, conversational, casual, etc.), the principal challenged the staff members with a newer form of communication: texting on their cell phones. The staff had to see who could text a given message the fastest. Everyone reacted instantly. Some texted, some watched, and some just laughed uproariously. While there was a winner to the contest, the staff members got the message that texting is fair game today as a communication method.

A principal modeled another contest that made its point about literacy quite easily when she asked her teacher teams to generate a list of words around the word *read*. She said, "People read . . ." and the teams had a relay at the board to list as many "things" we read as possible.

"We read . . . greens, music, words, phrases, faces, maps, charts, graphs, body language, codes, cereal boxes, sale tags, documents, tweeter messages, texts, textbooks, comics, symbols, and so on."

MORPH GRID II: STAFF MEETINGS

Captivate Strategy 10. Problem Based Learning (PBL) Scenarios

Explanation (What it is!)

A scenario is just that. It is a scene that is set up to create a feeling of being in the midst of the situation. It usually includes a "stakeholder role," or a point of view, and it describes the circumstances that surround that person or viewpoint. The scenario, of course, starts with a topic of concern. It is written as a broadly stated problem, ending with an open-ended question. It might sound like this: "You are a college student in a foreign country. You sense an anti-American sentiment wherever you go; yet as you get to know people individually, they are really very friendly and often very interested in knowing about America. You are eager to be accepted as an honorable representative of America. What will you do?"

Application (When to use it!)

Creating and resolving problem scenarios is an effective discussion strategy for staff members as they tackle a persistent problem or challenge. It puts the onus of responsibility on the participants and often turns a "gripe session" into a constructive problem solving session. There really isn't a best time for using the problem scenario, but it does make a robust and rich activity in the heart of the meeting. It gets teams really involved and invested in finding alternative solutions to chronic problems or solutions for immediate concerns that have just emerged.

Elaboration (How to use it!)

Here are several examples to illustrate what *Problem Based Learning Scenarios* might look like:

Data Scenario

Your grade-level team is expected to utilize student achievement data to determine flexible skill groupings for differentiated instruction. The problem is that you have so much data you are confused about where to start. What do you do?

Classroom Management Scenario

Several students take up all of your time. One is in constant need of reprimanding and you find yourself focusing your attention on him. Another won't participate in any way, and the third one has real learning problems that you feel you must address. What can you do?

Response to Intervention

Your PLC has been charged with the task of recommending appropriate literacy strategies for the three-tiered model of intervention:

Tier 1: whole group, Tier 2: small group, and Tier 3: individual

What will you do?

MORPH GRID II: STAFF MEETINGS

Captivate Strategy 11. D & D/Drop and Debrief

Explanation (What it is!)

One way to process and reflect on a completed assignment from a meeting is to have faculty teams use the *D & D/Drop and Debrief* strategy. In this strategy, teams pair up and take turns dropping their posters on the floor as everyone forms a half circle around the artifact. One team member explains what they have done. Then, the other team does the same. This allows two teams to talk and debrief, rather than the traditional sharing of each group's work with the entire room. It also fosters a little movement in the room to add some energy to the meeting. Drop and Debrief is a viable sharing strategy for teams to debrief on work they have done around an issue of concern.

Application (When to use it!)

Naturally, the Drop and Debrief strategy has to follow the work completed by partners or teams during the meeting. It is a useful way to get teachers involved and invested in generating their opinions through a visual that can be shared with others.

Once the D & D has occurred, the principal can sample the results from the groups by asking for teams to share a highlight from their debriefing. In this way, everyone in the room has an opportunity to hear about the range of ideas that were discussed more fully in the D & D groups.

Elaboration (How to use it!)

Examples of Drop and Debrief opportunities that might be used in a staff meeting include the following five ideas:

1. Teams create a graphic organizer, on poster paper, that depicts the topic of the meeting and then share it through a D & D.

2. Partners develop a T-chart of the pros and cons of the idea under discussion and compare and contrast it with a D & D.

3. PLCs design a visual metaphor to demonstrate their thinking on the concern under scrutiny, and then D & D to continue the conversation with another PLC.

4. Small groups jigsaw an issue, each taking a part of it, and then D & D their findings. A sampling of each group must occur to get the whole picture.

5. Individuals create a poster-sized log entry about the data they think is most significant, urgent, and able to get immediate impact (if addressed). Sharing by means of a D & D follows.

MORPH GRID II: STAFF MEETINGS

Captivate Strategy 12. Photo Story

Explanation (What it is!)

A *Photo Story* is exactly what it sounds like. It is a story created from photos from the digital photo program on your computer. In essence, you create a story from your photos in the program on your computer.

1. Open Microsoft Photo Story software—"Begin" a new story

2. Import and arrange your photos

3. Add text to the pictures—Font color

4. Voice Over—Narrate your pictures

5. Customize—Motion and transitions

6. Add background music

7. Save your story

Check out this Web site for help with PhotoStory 3: http://www.jakesonline.org/photostory.pdf.

Application (When to use it!)

The best way to use this strategy is to incorporate it as part and parcel of the meeting. It's a way to share curriculum standards for mapping purposes, instructional strategies for comparing, or even formative assessment work in the classroom. Each teacher or team would prepare a Photo Story prior to the meeting, and then several stories would be shared over the course of several meetings. The summary statements would then be elected to pull all of the ideas together.

Elaboration (How to use it!)

Using a computer to create a photo story is an effective way to demonstrate a point.

An example of a powerful way to get into the use of a Photo Story is to help each faculty member do a Photo Story of themselves. Then, they can share throughout the year, at the beginning of the faculty, grade-level, or department meetings.

Eventually, a Photo Story can be assembled to show how literacy is supported in every classroom or to demonstrate particular differentiation strategies for either the developing or advanced learner.

MORPH GRID II: STAFF MEETINGS

Close Strategy 1. Take Away Window

Explanation (What it is!)

A *Take Away Window* is simply a strategy list for teachers to have when they leave the meeting. By creating a take away list, the leader makes the strategies explicit. Rather than just using an activity in the meeting to help make a point, the strategy list makes it clear that this activity can be used many times in many situations, both in the staff room and in the classroom. An activity, in essence, becomes a generic strategy when it is applied broadly for different uses.

A graphic organizer, such as the attribute web, might be used in the meeting setting to list all of the methods teachers use to prep kids for a test. Yet when the attribute web is listed as a take away, it becomes an idea to revisit and use again. In turn, the web might be used another time in a faculty meeting, to generate ideas for successful parent conferences. In addition, teachers might use the web in a classroom science lesson to list all of the attributes of mammals, the atom, living things, or DNA. Suddenly the Take Away Window becomes a bank of ideas to take away and use again!

Application (When to use it!)

Have each staff member take away a list of ideas and strategies presented in the meeting by making a frame around a single sheet of paper to represent a window. Keep a list throughout the session as an explicit reminder of what to take away.

The idea of the Take Away Window transfers easily to the classroom for each lesson. Teachers simply create a Take Away Window on the board and place the objective, or take away, in the window as they say, "Today, the take away is adding double digit numbers," or, "Today, the take away is using specific 'charged' language to write persuasive essays."

Elaboration (How to use it!)

An example of a Take Away Window is displayed below. Notice that every single strategy is made explicit and listed precisely for later review.

TAKE AWAY WINDOW		
Graphic Organizer-Attribute Web	Note-Taking Foldable	Movement/Music
Think Pair Share	Brainstorming	Circle of Chairs
Summary Statement	HOT-Analysis	Take Away Window

MORPH GRID II: STAFF MEETINGS

Close Strategy 2. Mrs. Potter's Questions

Explanation (What it is!)

Mrs. Potter's Questions is a set of metacognitive, or reflective, questions that require thoughtful responses. These four questions delve into the *how* and *why* of an activity, rather than merely the *what*. As you can see, Mrs. Potter's Questions target reflection on the process, not on the content.

1. What were you trying to do?

2. What did you do well?

3. What might change if you did it again?

4. How might I help you?

Application (When to use it!)

Use Mrs. Potter's Questions at the end of an interaction in the staff meeting to get the teachers to think about how they worked together and what they did well, or might do differently, if they encountered the same task again.

Used with partners or in small groups, Mrs. Potter's Questions foster reflective conversations. This set of questions is a way to reflect on the meeting issues and how the teachers address the issues.

Naturally, the questions transfer easily into the classroom setting to get the students to become more reflective in their thinking.

Elaboration (How to use it!)

Ask staff members to discuss the four questions following a partner or small group activity, such as creating a "menu of services" that might be offered to students who need structured help with their homework. Once the teams have listed their ideas and debriefed the various lists from the different teams, have them talk through Mrs. Potter's Questions within their teams.

1. What were you trying to do? LIST IDEAS FOR HOMEWORK HELP

2. What did you do well? WE PRODUCED A LONG LIST

3. What might change if you did it again? MORE EVALUATION OF THE LIST

4. How might I help you? MAYBE A TIME WARNING WOULD HELP

MORPH GRID II: STAFF MEETINGS

Close Strategy 3. Reminder for Transfer

Explanation (What it is!)

A *Reminder for Transfer* is a touchback to the ideas of the meeting. It's a way to remind teachers that there are some ideas that were modeled throughout the meeting that have application in their classroom practices. The reminder is a lead-in, or stem statement, that fosters a mindful response about how the ideas might be used in a classroom example.

Reminder for Transfer

"The one strategy that we talked about today that I have never used, but will commit to using in the next month, is _____!"

"One idea that I am taking with me today is the _____. I know how I can use that in my lesson on _____. I am eager to see how the kids react to it."

Application (When to use it!)

Use this strategy following a meeting in which you have implicitly and explicitly modeled some active engaged-learning activities. *Implicit modeling* is when you simply use the strategy in the course of your meeting activities. *Explicit modeling* is when you use a strategy and give the *metacognitive monologue,* or what is referred to as "sharing the why." You might actually say, "Notice that I used the Think Pair Share to structure a conversation between partners. It is a great strategy to get the students thinking individually and then together."

Simply pass out a sheet of paper with the lead statement on it or have teachers write it on a sheet of paper. Ask them to talk with a partner about what they will do, and rather than collecting the papers, simply ask teachers to bring them back to the next meeting to share what they planned and what they did.

Elaboration (How to use it!)

A principal used the Reminder for Transfer strategy at the opening day staff meeting. He said, "Today I will be modeling several engaged learning strategies that I want you to notice. I will be doing this regularly at meetings to 'walk the walk' about engaged student learning methods. At the end of the meeting, I will ask you to select one strategy that you will deliberately use the first week of classes. We will go over the Reminder for Transfer statement to do that. Now, there may be many strategies that you already do, but I still want to 'model the model' in all of our meetings." He then hands them a sheet with the statement: "One strategy I will use is the _____," setting the stage for the year.

MORPH GRID II: STAFF MEETINGS

Close Strategy 4. Bookmark Think About

Explanation (What it is!)

A *Bookmark Think About* is a strip of paper, as you would imagine, that lists a number of ideas to take from the meeting. Teachers can use it as a real bookmark, placed in a plan book or log, to look at and review when appropriate.

The bookmark may be a handmade foldable or it may be prepared ahead of time as a laminated reminder of the key points of the meeting. It may list key phrases for higher-order questions to use throughout classroom discussions to cue more divergent, open-ended questions.

What might be an example of that?

How did you figure that out?

Why do you think that?

Will you cite a place in the text to support that idea?

Do you agree or disagree with that supposition?

Application (When to use it!)

Provide a laminated bookmark of the key points in the topic of the meeting, or have teachers create a bookmark with the essential elements. The bookmark makes an effective take away item that serves as a reminder of the issues that were discussed.

Elaboration (How to use it!)

Use the Bookmark Think About to "save for eternity" the key points of a discussion, an essential quote, or even a set of bullet points that cue a particular procedure.
Possible bookmark quote:

> The person doing
> the talking is
> the person doing
> the learning.

MORPH GRID II: STAFF MEETINGS

Close Strategy 5. Jingle

Explanation (What it is!)

A jingle is a great strategy to use in order to put energy into the meeting, to build teamwork, and to provide comic relief in the session. It is used to summarize the points made or to culminate other activities pursued in the meeting. The jingle might summarize what the PLCs' mission is all about:

(Sung to "Row, Row, Row Your Boat")

PLCs are here to stay.

PLCs are the way.

Heads together is the best.

Hands together does the rest.

Application (When to use it!)

In this strategy, the teams can wrap up a session by creating a jingle for their team. It almost becomes a contest of sorts, which teams can rally around.

While the jingles seem a little silly, it gets everyone on board as they try to complete the jingle. It is a bit of risk-taking that brings the team together, and it works well when the faculty shares the jingles with the other teams. Everyone laughs and appreciates the tunes, and there is a definite shift in the energy in the room.

Elaboration (How to use it!)

For example, when talking about how to foster application of learning, you can use the following:

"Little Bo Peep has lost her sheep,

And doesn't know where to find them.

Leave them alone, and they will come home,

Wagging their tails behind them."

This jingle says it all. It shows what can happen when we don't shepherd the transfer of learning. We can't just leave learning alone. We must talk about how to use the learning.

The jingles or nursery rhymes are tools used, metaphorically, as summaries to important ideas. Don't shy away from them. They work when you work with them.

MORPH GRID II: STAFF MEETINGS

Close Strategy 6. Shake and Break! I Appreciate!

Explanation (What it is!)

Shake and Break! I Appreciate! is a strategy to show appreciation to others on the team and to officially end an activity or a session. It is a physical gesture, well-recognized as a socially friendly way of acknowledging others. Just by saying, "Shake and Break! Shake hands across the way, side by side, and kitty-corner. Tell your teammates how much you appreciate their contributions today," the leader models desired social behavior for effective teamwork.

Application (When to use it!)

One way to bring closure to an activity or to the meeting is to use the Shake and Break! I Appreciate! activity. As already mentioned, ask the teachers or staff members to shake hands—side by side, across the way, and kitty-corner. Ask them to go around the group and give an, "I appreciate...," to a team member or to the team as a whole.

Eventually, and over time, this kind of appreciation activity becomes part of the norms established for the staff meeting, the PLC, or even the classroom. It is a management tool that focuses on honoring the ideas of others and appreciating the differences in others. It is important in staff room interactions and also in classroom practices.

Elaboration (How to use it!)

For example...

"I appreciate your humor, Bob. You diffused the tension we were all feeling at one point, and it allowed us to move on."

"I really liked the way you kept us on track, Sarah. You kept bringing us back to the key points when we would wander into other areas."

"Joe, you have a wonderful way of helping us all see the value of these decisions."

MORPH GRID II: STAFF MEETINGS

Close Strategy 7. Ms. Poindexter's Questions

Explanation (What it is!)

This is a problem-solving strategy that can permeate staff room situations. *Ms. Poindexter's Questions* ask those in the meeting to reflect on a moment when they were stuck on the issue and to talk about how they got unstuck. The questions are simply,

Where did you get stuck?

How did you get unstuck?

In the process of using these questions as a discussion technique, the tide turns from strident positions, in which opposing viewpoints stand strong, to yielding positions that signal compromise. It is important to understand that we often get stuck on an idea or in a situation and that we all develop a set of problem solving strategies that work for us in many situations. These are highly respected reflection questions.

Application (When to use it!)

It's a life lesson to know that everyone gets stuck. Everyone has a moment—in doing a project, undertaking an investigation, or even in thinking about particular issues—when they are puzzled about what to do next. Why not promote this kind of honest appraisal of progress and openly share how, when, and where we get stuck and how, when, and where we manage to get unstuck.

Elaboration (How to use it!)

One example of how to use Ms. Poindexter's Questions comes from a true story that happened during a doctoral defense session. The doctoral candidate was asked by one of the professors on her committee, "During your dissertation journey, describe where you got stuck and how you got unstuck."

Surprised that the professor knew that she had gotten really stuck at one point about how to manage and analyze the mountain of observational and anecdotal data she had accumulated, she asked this question of him, following the session, "Professor, I was wondering how you knew I had gotten stuck?"

He smiled and replied, "Everyone gets stuck! Didn't you know that?"

MORPH GRID II: STAFF MEETINGS

Close Strategy 8. Art Journal

Explanation (What it is!)

An art journal is a powerful, multimodal tool to use to get staff to think about their ideas in a visual way. These might be graphic organizers, thinking maps, graphs, charts, drawings, sketches, doodles, cartoons, or illustrations. It is a strategy to move away from words and to show, visually, the gist of the meeting. It models the strategies of a differentiated classroom and, at the same time, models differentiation in the staff room.

Application (When to use it!)

Ask staff members to draw their representation of the day's meeting issues and to share them with a partner. Use this at the end of the discussion as a culminating activity. It really does tend to pull things together as they strive to find a visual way of communicating their thoughts.

The art journal is also a highly effective tool to use in the classroom to motivate students to reflect in a visual mode, rather than in a purely verbal way.

Elaboration (How to use it!)

SEE IT! SAY IT! DO IT!
THE MULTIMODAL WAY TO DIFFERENTIATE

MORPH GRID II: STAFF MEETINGS

Close Strategy 9. Prizes

Explanation (What it is!)

The strategy of giving out prizes as an incentive or as a motivational tactic is as old as the ages. The prize can be given to the first person to arrive, to each grade level or department, or as a random drawing. The prizes can be common supplies that teachers need (markers, sticky notes, stickers, note paper, etc.), everyday treats (candy, gum, coupons, etc.), or even relevant materials (books, booklets, pamphlets, etc.). It does not matter what the prizes are; they are always appreciated, and they definitely create an aura of excitement and fun.

Application (When to use it!)

Have a prize for a giveaway right after the lunch break as an incentive to get the people back on time, or at the end of a session as a closing rally point. Show the prizes; play up the drama because most people get pretty excited about winning a prize.

Estimate how many people there are in the room and use that number as a range for the "secret numbers."

Say, "Everyone think of a number between 1 and 75. Write it down somewhere, and do not show your neighbor." Then, the presenter says, "I will call out several numbers. If I call your number, you win the prize. Just come up and get your prize."

Participants then select from the prizes offered.

Elaboration (How to use it!)

Several examples of prizes that were given to teachers at the meeting include the following:

1. One principal gave away five copies of the book *inFormative Assessment: When It's Not About a Grade* at the staff meeting. The strategy served as a follow up and reminder of the PD session that had occurred the week before.

2. Another example of a "prized" prize was when a principal gave away Opening Day tickets to the Cubs game at Wrigley Field.

3. The prize of coupons redeemable at the local craft store was also a popular gift for teachers at one elementary school, while the high school teachers got excited about the prizes that centered around another kind of coupon—a coupon for coverage of one study hall or one lunch duty, and so on.

MORPH GRID II: STAFF MEETINGS

Close Strategy 10. Highlights! Insights!

Explanation (What it is!)

Highlights/Insights is a cueing strategy to stimulate reflective thinking about something that was targeted in the staff meeting. It is a metacognitive cue for highlights about the actual topic under discussion and for insights that occurred as the discussion unfolded. In short, the two questions cover the whole of the discussion summary:

Highlights—cognitive points

Insights—reflective connections

"One highlight for me was when I understood the concept of transfer of learning that we talked about. It gave me insight into the idea that I need to be looking for transfer with my students."

Application (When to use it!)

Toward the close of the meeting, a quick, yet comprehensive, way to reflect on the meeting focus is to ask the staff to work in pairs and to respond to two arenas: the highlights of the meeting and the insights taken away from the discussion. While it creates a dynamic way to close the meeting, this strategy can also be used during a particular segment of the meeting. It's a way to end one part and then transition into the next part.

Elaboration (How to use it!)

An example of using this simple, yet effective, reflection can be seen in the story of a principal who wanted to talk about the building test scores as a way of opening up the conversation about what the staff might do differently. He said, "We have been looking at data for seven years and nothing has changed. My conclusion is that either we don't know how to teach reading and math, or we're not doing something right with the data we have. Which one do you think it is? Talk it over and let's share highlights and insights from our discussions."

After much discussion in pairs and small groups, a seasoned staff member stood up and said, "A highlight for me was hearing the stark facts: we have not changed our scores in seven years. An insight I've had is that we look at the data and then go back and try to work on 'comprehension' or 'problem solving,' or whatever the data indicates, but we don't really do anything differently than we have done before. That is why we get the same results. We need a focused way to go back and work smarter, not just harder, if we are going to get different results."

MORPH GRID II: STAFF MEETINGS

Close Strategy 11. Staircase

Explanation (What it is!)

The *Staircase* is a highly creative strategy that requires both creative and critical thinking skills. It is a structured brainstorm of words to illuminate the meaning and the multiple facets of the topic. The participants, as partners or teams, create an inverted pyramid of words that all begin with the same letter and increase in length by one letter as they are shaped to fit the model.

Topic:	Management
	M
	Me
	Map
	More
	Messy
	Manage

Application (When to use it!)

Have teams or pairs generate a staircase of words as a closure to the meeting topic, as suggested by the brief model above. You can use the same letter for each group to create a concert of ideas, or you can change the letter for each group to make it more challenging.

While the brainstorm part is easy, it really takes a lot of revising to get the proper words in the proper spot. It is a challenge that elicits teamwork and, sometimes, a sense of competition.

Elaboration (How to use it!)

It might look like this example, which was created following a meeting on data.

PLCs	*Integrated*	*Technology*
D		T
Do		To
Did		Two
Data		Team
Doing		Teach
Dialog		Themes
Discuss		Toggles
Database		

MORPH GRID II: STAFF MEETINGS

Close Strategy 12. Energizers

Explanation (What it is!)

Energizers, or *Hurrahs*, are simple, little, funny, and, yes, hokey cheers performed by the group members to create a new energy in the room. Many times, the staff meeting occurs at the end of a day, when teachers are fatigued from the demands of the classroom. The energizers revive the group.

Energizers can also be used efficiently to show appreciation for a group reporting back on a task. Again, they truly do energize the group—everyone gets into it and laughs nervously as they perform the cheer. It's up to the leader to take the lead. Try them, even if it seems a little uncomfortable. Lead the cheer with confidence and you'll be surprised by how well it catches on. It's all in the delivery. Go for It!

Application (When to use it!)

The list of Energizers is used to provide a moment of celebration to energize adults with a little rhythm and movement. Each one has its own special flavor. See Appendix B for more instructions and hand gestures that go along with the cheers. Here is the list:

Cowboy Cheer	Cheese and Grater
Shine Your Halo	Elvis Cheer
Olé! Olé! Olé!	Fantastic
Hamburger Cheer	Rattlesnake Cheer
Sign Language	Saturday Night Fever
Applause	Seal of Approval
A-W-E-S-O-M-E	Harry Potter Cheer
Firecracker	A "Round" of Applause
Hip-Hip-Hooray	Wow!
Pat Yourself on the Back	Gold Star Class
Lookin' Good	I Like It!
Trucker Cheer	

Elaboration (How to use it!)

Use the cheers to model for the classroom. When kids are in class all day long, they need moments of movement and levity. These help them refocus on the next learning activity with a renewed interest and concentration.

3

Morph Grid III

Leading Professional Learning Communities

INTRODUCTION

Professional Learning Communities (PLCs), by virtue of their full name, are conceived, designed, and implemented in K–12 schools around the globe to provide collegial centers for teachers. By targeting student success through professional collaborations, the PLC is a natural organization for promoting more reflective practice. PLCs offer staff a golden opportunity to epitomize the lifelong learner.

From Staff Room to Classroom II: The One-Minute Professional Development Planner features any number of tools and techniques to enhance the PLC session with practical and transferable strategies for the staff room and classroom.

DIRECTIONS

Roll a set of dice three times to select an activity for the three elements based on the numbers rolled. Be courageous and go with the actual numbers. Don't cheat. It will make your PLCs lively, original, and effective.

1. *Capture* the staff members' attention: Openers.

2. *Captivate* with the "meat of the meeting."

3. *Close* with keepers.

CATEGORICAL LISTING OF ALL MORPH TOOLS

Check Appendix A for an index of strategies by type of tool (e.g., collaborative tool or management tool).

CREATIVE OPTIONS

Remember, the strategies are interchangeable and often work as any of the three elements, depending on the context and how they are used. An opener may be used as a closer or even as part of the "meat" of the session. Be creative and use the grid of strategies with your own creative flair.

MORPH GRID III: LEADING PLCs

Capture Strategy 1. 2-4-8 Focus Interview

Explanation (What it is!)

This is a speaking-listening interaction. The strategy of the *2-4-8 Focus Interview* encourages active speaking and attentive listening roles that are at the heart of collegial PLC conversations. As the team leader, have the team follow these steps:

2—Begin with A and B partners and C and D partners. Have the A partners share with the B partners about a memorable item. The C and D partners should do the same.

4—Then have the A and B partners join the C and D partners. The A partner tells the B partner's story. The B partner tells the A partner's story. The C partner tells D's story, and the D partner tells the C partner's story.

8—Now, if there is time, each group of four should match up with another group of four to form a group of eight. Each person must tell a third partner's story. At this point, the stories are quite short as each person has just a little information.

Application (When to use it!)

The 2-4-8 Focus Interview is welcomed as an opening activity to get teachers talking and sharing. It sets the stage in a partnership, and then in a small group of four, it allows the teachers to share ideas in a comfortable environment. The 2-4-8 activity is also a great way to summarize ideas in a second meeting, as a reaction to the input from an earlier session.

Elaboration (How to use it!)

The PLC team members can use the 2-4-8 Focus Interview (or 2-4 if more appropriate for the numbers) to share student artifacts from a designated or specific engaged learning lesson. For example, if the team is focusing on problem-solving skills, each department member or cross-departmental team member would bring one lesson sample to share.

For the classroom, the primary example is using the 2-4-8 for a show and tell activity, in which the items are shared first by the owners and then again by the listeners. "Here is my favorite comic book. I love Batman because he helps others." Then, in the foursome, "Tommy brought his Batman comic, his favorite comic book, telling how Batman does good for the world."

Similarly, an upper-level classroom example is to use the 2-4-8 Focus Interview to share book reports by displaying a poster of the book and then telling and retelling in the 2-4-8 format of active speaking and attentive listening.

MORPH GRID III: LEADING PLCs

Capture Strategy 2. People Search

Explanation (What it is!)

The *People Search* is sometimes regarded as merely a mixer or icebreaker activity, yet it is a powerful and viable engaging-discussion tool for the PLC. A People Search consists of a set of 8 to 10 statements about a topic of concern. The statements should be open-ended to encourage discussion between team members. For the PLC, *data, grades, study habits,* and *test-taking strategies* are appropriate and possible topics.

Once the statements are developed, teachers move about the room to find someone who will respond to a particular statement. Then, they reverse roles and the other partner responds to a question or statement. After they have both responded and engaged in the conversation, they initial each other's sheet and move on to another person.

Application (When to use it!)

Use the People Search as a no-fail opening activity, and it does act as an icebreaker or mixer. However, by adding substantive questions or statements around a relevant topic, the real essence of the discussion starter is tapped.

Elaboration (How to use it!)

Example Topic: Data
Find someone who...

1. will share a piece of data about themselves.

2. compares hard data with soft data.

3. agrees or disagrees with data-driven instruction.

4. hasn't been on a data in a long time.

5. describes the value of observational and anecdotal data.

6. ranks hard and soft data the same as you do.

7. declares a quantitative statement of fact about their student data.

8. considers themselves data savvy and will tell you why.

Take a moment to debrief after teachers have had time to chat with each other. Sample some of the responses.

MORPH GRID III: LEADING PLCs

Capture Strategy 3. Agree/Disagree—Think Pair Share

Explanation (What it is!)

The *Agree/Disagree—Think Pair Share* sheet consists of 10 to 15 statements about a target topic. It is sometimes called an *Agree/Disagree Anticipation Guide,* in which statements are answered in response to the anticipated information. Used in this way, the Agree/Disagree is a prelearning strategy that stirs up prior knowledge and background information.

Using a *Think Pair Share* activity, ask teachers to *think* and respond to the statements with a "+" (plus) if they agree, and a "−" (minus) if they disagree. Then, have *pairs* scan their respective responses and talk about the ones that don't match. Have them try to come to a shared opinion. Debrief by sampling a few items that are of grave concern to the group.

Application (When to use it!)

Use this as a prior knowledge piece to begin discussion on a topic of interest and concern at the start of the PLC meeting. This gives members a way to ease into the discussion and to rehearse their thoughts on the topic before they are front and center in the discussion.

It is also interesting to revisit the Agree/Disagree activity following the meeting or in a subsequent meeting in order to see how opinions or views might have shifted and changed. Thus, this also makes a great postlearning strategy.

Elaboration (How to use it!)

Example Agree/Disagree. Topic: Test Prep

1. Test prep is a "must do."

2. All students benefit from test-taking strategies.

3. Most teachers have "tricks of the trade" for tests.

4. Test prep takes too much class time.

5. Many students don't test well, in spite of test prep.

6. Teach for a lifetime, not for a test!

7. Students are immune to test prep because they don't see the value in it.

8. The most valuable part of test prep is the logistics, not the content.

9. Parents can also benefit from test prep activities.

10. Learning time must take precedent over testing time.

MORPH GRID III: LEADING PLCs

Capture Strategy 4. T-Chart

Explanation (What it is!)

The *T-Chart* is a well-known and well-worn graphic organizer that is used to delineate two related ideas. The T-Chart is used in a number of ways: pros and cons listing, a looks like and sounds like description, or a comparing and contrasting activity. Simply make a large *T* on a sheet of paper, with two columns and a place for the headings. Then, individually, in pairs, or in teams, complete the chart by generating ideas for each column.

Used in a PLC format, the T-Chart might list the pros and cons of PLCs. The T-Chart might also list what an engaged learning classroom looks like and sounds like. Using the T-Chart to compare and contrast two comprehension strategies or two different problem-solving strategies is an effective way to unpack the two ideas for further scrutiny.

Application (When to use it!)

The T-Chart is a good opening activity to get the thinking going and to examine various viewpoints that occur in PLCs as they discuss pertinent issues. It gets the ball rolling in pairs and partner work.

The T-Chart can also be used as a discussion exercise for preparing for a debate on a controversial issue that has emerged within the PLC group talking points. It makes a clarifying tool by exposing the hidden details of a concern or issue.

Elaboration (How to use it!)

Here is an example of starting a T-chart on the issue of parent conferences. This concern came up after a discussion of the time and energy spent on these conferences and the poor turnout of parents at the high school level.

Topic: Parent Conferences	
PROS	CONS
Get to meet parents	Takes time to prepare
Two-way conversation	Student presence
Students-led brings parents	Poor attendance

MORPH GRID III: LEADING PLCs

Capture Strategy 5. Tri-Fold Brochure

Explanation (What it is!)

The *Tri-Fold Brochure* is simply a piece of paper folded in three vertical sections, much like a little brochure or flyer of information. Creating a Tri-Fold Brochure as a PLC is an effective way of communicating with parents, students, or even other staff members. The focus is always a pressing concern, and the flyer becomes the messenger of whatever information you want to communicate. The ideas in a brochure take on a certain stature. "Oh, the information must be important and lasting. It's in a professional looking brochure. It must be a keeper."

Application (When to use it!)

Take time in the PLC meeting to sketch out what you, as a group, want desperately to communicate to others—to parents, to students, to the administration, or even to other PLCs in the building or across the district.

Use this as an opening activity to ruminate, delineate, and illuminate thinking on an issue or concern. It gives structure to the thinking and the discussion that ensues. It acts as an advance organizer and keeps the conversation and remarks on track. Just deciding on how to organize the ideas into three columns generates a lot of talk about the labels for the three sections. In the end, these are the important labels that help to organize the many ideas on the table.

Elaboration (How to use it!)

After discussion about the increasing problem with "no homework done," this PLC decided to lay out all of the concerns and to develop a positive memo in the form of a Tri-Fold Brochure to share their concerns with parents.

Here is an example of what the teacher team began to develop in a brochure to parents and students about the various roles played in the homework policy:

Homework Policies		
Teacher	*Student*	*Parent*
Assign	Do	Support
Check	Revisit	Discuss

MORPH GRID III: LEADING PLCs

Capture Strategy 6. Facts and Fun—Partner Introduction

Explanation (What it is!)

The *Facts and Fun—Partner Introduction* is a strategy for getting to know the members of the PLC in more depth. In this activity, partners share information about each other by preparing a one-minute introduction. The introductions to others should include key facts and vital statistics about the person in order to establish their credibility as a professional. In addition, the introduction should include an interesting anecdote about the human side of the person to make the introduction both more personable and more memorable. It is well-known that people remember stories more easily than they remember stark facts.

Application (When to use it!)

The introduction is an opening activity to get everyone comfortable and feeling at ease. It is a fun and high-energy method to use to begin the session. Even when everyone knows each other, it is interesting to find a tidbit to share about a partner as you introduce him or her to the group for that session. It recognizes every teacher there as a valued member of the PLC team.

In the end, it sets a precedent for similar classroom behavior, honoring team members in the various task groups the teacher may set up. Introductions are part and parcel of the social scene of working groups. It is a good practice to practice.

Elaboration (How to use it!)

Sample introduction of a fellow PLC member:

Phil is a pillar of Bloomfield High. He has been here for seventeen years and, as you all know, is the esteemed head of the chemistry department. One of his greatest achievements has been in his advocacy of the AP programs, which have increased by 50% over the past five years. Just to add a note of humor, Phil tells the story often about how kids say, "Chemistry stinks!" And he adds, "They're right. Chemistry definitely has its own set of odors. It's funny, but that's part of what I love about my chem. lab."

MORPH GRID III: LEADING PLCs

Capture Strategy 7. Line Up Lanes

Explanation (What it is!)

*Line Up Lane*s is a management tool for moving people into a new team for a new task. The leader can employ clever ways of mixing and matching team members in an effort to establish a bonding of sorts and to build team spirit as the PLC prepares to get down to work. For one session, the team members can line up by birthdays from January to December. For another session, they can line up alphabetically by last names or even by height, from the tallest to the shortest. You get the idea. Each time, the members are assigned to the people next to them or across from them, or whatever creative idea works, so they are changing the teams to change the dynamics.

It sounds a little silly when you may have a PLC consisting of four or five people, but it is often true that we tend to sit by and talk to the same people at every meeting. We are creatures of habit and we need explicit strategies to break out of the mold.

Application (When to use it!)

This is often used with large groups, but as mentioned above, it works just as well with small groups. Of course, it is a great way to start the meeting, but it also can be used as a transition to change activities. Use Line Up Lanes whenever you think it will energize and liven up the group. It's fun, and at the same time, we often learn new things about the people we are working with.

Elaboration (How to use it!)

Line Up Lanes that work:

Line up by birthday months, years of experience, number of children, favorite season of the year, pizza preference, seniority at the school, favorite beverages, and so on. It's fun and it gets people talking and laughing before they get down to business.

One example of Line Up Lanes is a PLC leader asking the members to line up by the last four digits of their Social Security number—just to jog their memories of that number, which is asked so often.

MORPH GRID III: LEADING PLCs

Capture Strategy 8. Memory Pegs

Explanation (What it is!)

Memory Pegs are physical cues or hand and body motions, if you will, that "peg" a word or thought to help the person remember the information. According to brain science, muscle memory is one of the memory channels in the human brain. This procedural memory is accessed in the cerebellum. It is a powerful memory system that we can model in the PLC meeting for later transfer and use in classroom learning.

Folklore also supports brain science. The concept that physical hand cues are powerful memory pegs is as old as the ages. Think about the nursery rhymes and limericks that you learned as a toddler and the hand cues that went with them. Try saying "Itsy Bitsy Spider" without using the hand motions that go with "up the water spout."

Application (When to use it!)

Use Memory Pegs as a catalyst for remembering key facts at the beginning of the session that will be used throughout the meeting that day. Use four Memory Pegs to recall the four data questions that PLC teams talk through or walk through as they unpack the data and plan interventions.

What? (Make a question mark with your index finger)

What else? (Point to the side of your forehead)

So what? (Open hands and shrug shoulders)

Now what? (Shake index finger)

Elaboration (How to use it!)

For example, there are four generations of adults working in our schools—Veterans, Baby Boomers, Gen Xers, and Millennials—so the PLC may consist of a mix of all four generations.

Try these hand signals to recall the four categories.

Veterans: Old timers; vibrant and wise; tech wannabe's . . . Tap watch

Baby Boomers: Rewarded; thriving; tech know-how . . . Hands up/fingers open

Gen Xers: Latch key kids; independent; tech-savvy . . . Turn key

Millennials: Cared for "youngens"; fun loving; tech in the DNA . . . Hug self

MORPH GRID III: LEADING PLCs

Capture Strategy 9. MI Grid

Explanation (What it is!)

The *MI Grid,* or *Multiple Intelligences Grid,* presents a grid of the eight intelligences with a series of activities listed for each of them. By moving horizontally across the MI Grid, the leader can plan activities for the session that tap into the various modalities of the PLC team. It is an effective way to get teachers on board.

Here is a listing of what Howard Gardner (1983) identified as eight intelligences that human beings harbor in highly individual and varied profiles. Use this acronym: V-V-I-I-M-M-N-B, which stands for (vim n' b . . . sort of like "vim n' vigor") to recall the eight.

V Verbal/linguistic

V Visual/spatial

I Interpersonal/social

I Intrapersonal/self

M Mathematical/logical

M Musical/rhythmic

N Naturalistic/physical world

B Bodily/kinesthetic

Application (When to use it!)

The MI Grid is helpful when planning a PLC session, but it is also a great model to develop with the PLC when talking about differentiated curriculum, Response to Intervention, tiered learning strategies, or when facilitating flexible skill groups. The grid provides a bank of multimodal learning strategies to use at any time within the framework of classroom task teams or staff room PLC teams.

Elaboration (How to use it!)

Develop a grid of activities to choose from for different situations.

Verbal	Visual	Inter	Intra	Math	Music	Naturalist	Body
essay	picture	pairs	journal	compute	songs	flora	action
poem	graphic	trios	log	calculate	music	fauna	modeling
paragraph	table	partners	diary	problems	instrument	environment	doing
letter	chart	buddies	goals	equations	appreciate	"green"	making
text	sketch	team	p. best	formulas	perform	pollute	building

MORPH GRID III: LEADING PLCs

Capture Strategy 10. Deck of Cards

Explanation (What it is!)

The *Deck of Cards* strategy is an instructional best practice that provides a format for equal opportunity to respond. Even though the PLC is often smaller in numbers (4–6 members) rather than larger (6–12 members), it is still common for some people to talk much more frequently than others. This strategy ensures that every person gets a "spot and a slot" to respond.

Have two identical decks of cards. Use one deck as members walk into the meeting room. Give each person one to three cards, and ask them to look at the cards and keep them handy. Explain that, throughout the meeting, you will periodically pull a card from the second deck and ask the matching cardholder to comment. To alleviate any tensions, assure them that they can always say, "I pass," and you will move right on to the next card in your deck.

Application (When to use it!)

The Deck of Cards is a powerful technique to use at the start of every meeting. It soon becomes part of the norms set by the PLC—that everyone is expected to participate fully and will, in fact, be called upon to do so.

Share the idea that you are modeling this high-energy way to also keep students tuned in to the classroom setting.

Elaboration (How to use it!)

An example of the Deck of Cards strategy that was effective in a PLC meeting was modeled as people were asked to weigh in on their opinion about a particular "reading in the content area" strategy, called *SQ3R* (Survey, Question, Read, Recite, Review). The strategy was demonstrated and participants were asked if they felt that they knew this strategy well enough to incorporate it into the class time devoted to textbook reading, and they were also asked if they thought it was worthwhile to do.

As the PLC leader pulled one card after another from the deck, each person responded in detail about his or her confidence level with the strategy and his or her opinion about its value in helping kids comprehend the text.

MORPH GRID III: LEADING PLCs

Capture Strategy 11. Punch Line/Circle Back Stories

Explanation (What it is!)

The *Punch Line/Circle Back Stories* strategy is what is known as the "inside joke." It often occurs spontaneously within the course of events as the PLC meeting unfolds. Once this punch line or clever comment occurs, it can be referenced throughout subsequent meetings because everyone inside the group understands what it means.

A punch line emerged from a PLC when the leader said, "I want to 'share the why' on this point so we will all understand completely why we must adhere to this policy." From his discussion on "fidelity to the intervention," the punch line, "share the why," became a common phrase. Others used it in the PLC meetings when they wanted to make a salient and somber point that all should honor and respect.

Application (When to use it!)

This strategy is set up in the beginning of the meeting. After telling a story or joke that illustrates a key point, you return to the key point by relating new ideas or connections to the punch line. It is a thread that seems to weave through the entirety of the sessions and "insiders" get it immediately. It's almost like a code, but it is part of the bonding of the PLCs.

Elaboration (How to use it!)

For example, the presenter, explaining *transfer of learning* as being the ability of the learner to unconsciously apply new learning in new situations, tells the following story:

I was working with English language learners, helping them move beyond rote learning and simple memorization of sentences in English. I wanted them to apply the rules of English grammar and understand the differences between English and Spanish. I knew that they would really "know" their new language when they were able to apply what they had learned naturally. After working with a group of fifth graders off and on for a few weeks, one little girl looked up from her English reading assignment and said, "I am beginning to think in English!"

"I am thinking in English!" becomes the punch line that the leader returns to throughout the meeting. If, while facilitating groups, a member makes a comment that tells the leader that they do understand, then the leader says, "I am beginning to think you are thinking in English!"

MORPH GRID III: LEADING PLCs

Capture Strategy 12. Quiz

Explanation (What it is!)

The almighty quiz is the one of the oldest and most traditional incentives for learning. The Friday spelling quiz, the weekly current events quiz, and the monthly geography quiz are the check-up assessment tools most remember from their schooling days. Most remember that they "crammed" for the quiz. They reviewed and studied because they did not want to get a bad grade.

Well, believe it or not, PLCs can use the quiz just as effectively. Of course, the stakes are not perceived to be as high as they are for young students, but the quiz does put an onus of responsibility on the adult learner, just as it does for the young student.

Application (When to use it!)

There's nothing like that announced quiz to keep students on their toes. The same is true of the teachers in the PLC. A quick quiz on terms or concepts that are the focus of the PLC work can be invigorating. The quiz also acts as a revisit or review, as a boot up for the meeting to remind everyone of where they left off last time.

Elaboration (How to use it!)

The following is an example:

Whiz Quiz on Formative Assessment

1. Formative assessments should always be graded.

2. Define formative and summative assessments.

3. Show how the two assessments differ using a Venn diagram.

It's short and sweet and to the point! It puts everyone on notice that the information is important to the work of the PLC. It also has an element of fun to it. The quiz is an effective tool to use over and over again—because it works! It can be a simple true or false, a multiple-choice, or in that nagging essay format. Yet whatever it is, it will be a winning strategy to use.

MORPH GRID III: LEADING PLCs

Captivate Strategy 1. Turn to Your Partner and (TTYPA) . . . With a Shoulder Partner/Elbow Partner

Explanation (What it is!)

Turn to Your Partner and . . ., or *TTYPA . . .*, is a dialogue tool that is a quick way for the members to make sense of what is being said or presented. It's short and sweet, but addresses the brain science that implies that after 7 to 10 minutes, the brain needs to connect with the incoming stimuli in order to understand and internalize the new information. TTYPA . . . allows the teachers to reflect on the input and interpret, in a personal way, the essence of the idea. Turn to Your Partner and . . . is that moment of respite when the incoming information stops and the learners let the ideas percolate.

Application (When to use it!)

When giving a lot of information in a one-way broadcast, or in a lecture mode, Turn to Your Partner and . . . becomes an essential interactive strategy. TTYPA . . . , whether it is with a *Shoulder Partner* or an *Elbow Partner,* as previously determined, gives PLC members a chance to make sense of the input through the partner dialogue.

Use this throughout the meeting to add vital time to digest information through the dialogue with another. The person talking is internalizing the ideas through a cognitive rehearsal, while the listener is anchoring the information through active listening and subsequent dialogue.

Elaboration (How to use it!)

One clever example of the TTYPA . . . strategy is illustrated when the PLC leader completes a YouTube viewing of a piece titled "Shift Happens." In the video sequence, the ideas and images fly by the screen at a rapid rate, imitating the speed of the changing world. The viewers are bombarded with information about population demographics, technology, global issues, and language preferences as it represents the world as a global village. Teachers involved in this interaction need time to chew on the ideas that are presented in fleeting images. TTYPA . . . does the trick; it gives the viewers temporary relief as they talk through some of the ideas that were noted.

MORPH GRID III: LEADING PLCs

Captivate Strategy 2. CL Pointer Game/Roles and Responsibilities

Explanation (What it is!)

The *CL Pointer Game* is a management tool that helps the leader of the PLC set up roles for the team tasks that they will complete. The leader orchestrates the CL Pointer Game. She or he asks everyone in the group to arm themselves with their pointer finger, and on the count of three, to point to someone in the group. That person becomes "It," and the leader begins assigning the roles by naming one role for "It." Roles typically include some or all of the following, depending on the size of the team: Materials Manager, Recorder, Reporter, Encourager, and Time Keeper.

Application (When to use it!)

In the heat of the action, cooperative learning groups often work best with assigned roles to provide the needed structure to proceed efficiently. During the session, when a collaborative PLC task is needed, the assignment of roles and responsibilities ensures that everyone is on board and participating fully. It is also a way to change the traditional roles for each team member. Some are naturally gifted spokespersons, while others may prefer to record the information. By using the Pointer Game and assigning roles randomly, every member has the opportunity and responsibility to perform in roles outside their comfort zone. It really helps build shared leadership of the PLC.

Elaboration (How to use it!)

Using the Pointer Game in a data discussion session, the PLC leader assigned several data-savvy roles and responsibility:

1. Data Detective—Find the significant data in the documents

2. Data Coder—Assign the code to the data as the discussion unfolds (+ Strength, – Weakness, = Pattern, ! Surprise, ? Question)

3. Data Discusser—Lead the data dialogue and discussion

4. Data Doctor—Write the diagnosis and prescription for the data

Captivate Strategy 3. Carousel! Show and Tell!

Explanation (What it is!)

Carousel! Show and Tell! is a sharing strategy for the PLC, or for several PLCs. By establishing stations around the room, various groups or teams can do one designated part of the work on poster papers taped to the wall or on easels. Once the groups are finished, the entire PLC team "carousels" around from station to station in order to view the work and to hear the presentation by the group who owns the work. It is a powerful way to have everyone become involved in unpacking ideas and generating solutions to a concern of the PLC.

Application (When to use it!)

The Carousel! Show and Tell! is an appropriate strategy to use whenever there are several aspects or parts to a task. When the PLC leader has divided the work into several different tasks, this strategy is a wonderfully effective way to share the information that has been developed by the various subgroups within the PLC.

This powerful strategy offers recognition and time to show and tell, as well as movement and interaction, which creates its own energy in the meeting. Also, by putting the finished work up on the walls or on easels, it is displayed for everyone to see and to continue to review.

Elaboration (How to use it!)

For example, one PLC had four sets of partners work at their independent stations on finding alternative ways to get high school students involved in extracurricular activities. These were ideas to motivate them to stay in school and, in turn, decrease the drop-out rates. Moving around to the four stations, the PLC maximized the effort with multiple ideas to implement.

Ideas ranged from relevant and desired incentives, to buddy-relationship building, to creating a video showcasing the various extracurricular activities available to the student body. In the end, the team decided to implement all of the ideas over a scheduled plan. Each month they featured one of the ideas with the students.

MORPH GRID III: LEADING PLCs

Captivate Strategy 4. Mr. Pete's Questions and Cues

Explanation (What it is!)

Mr. Pete's Questions and Cues are probing and delving questions to provide depth and breadth to the development of an idea. One of the easiest ways to go beyond the one-word answer in a discussion format is to probe a bit further with some simple question cues:

1. Tell me more!

2. Give me an example!

3. Connect that to this idea!

While these are simple tools, they do indeed foster more in-depth thinking and more robust responses. Just by saying "Tell me more," the respondent often goes from that original one-word response to a complete paragraph of meaning.

Application (When to use it!)

Use these cues to encourage more comprehensive discussions throughout the PLC sessions. In fact, if the PLC leader models these question cues during each and every meeting discussion, they will become part of the discussion and debriefing norms for the group. Thus, discussions will become more meaty, more robust, and richer in context and content.

The meaty part is uncovering all of the facts, while the robustness comes from the full exposure of every member's opinion. Finally, the richness emerges as the team members go beyond the surface information and the superficial ideas to a deeper and more comprehensive picture of the situation. This is when the PLC discussions show evidence of mature and honest discussions that have the integrity of insights and innuendo.

Elaboration (How to use it!)

"Tell me more about that idea for our awards assembly. What exactly would that look like if it played out?"

"Well, it would mean that the student body would be responsible for scouting opportunities for giving awards to their peer groups. We would give them some categories and they would have a timeline in which to nominate candidates for the various awards. For example, we might have a Good Citizen Award, a Most Effort Recognition Certificate, and a Big Brother or Big Sister Award. You guys probably can think of lots of others that would be meaningful to the kids and their parents."

MORPH GRID III: LEADING PLCs

Captivate Strategy 5. Menu of Ideas—Appetizers/Meal/Dessert

Explanation (What it is!)

A *Menu of Ideas* is simply a listing of ideas that PLCs develop. In fact, the development of a Menu of Ideas for students is a worthy activity for the PLCs as they get started on their mission to serve the needs of their students. The focus of the menu can revolve around various concerns that were revealed through the student achievement data or other demographic data from the grade, department, or school level. Following along with the menu metaphor, the list often includes "appetizers" or simple things to do; the "main meal," or more robust ideas; and "desserts," or extras that are available for students.

Application (When to use it!)

Use this Menu of Ideas metaphor to brainstorm ideas whenever the PLC team is working on a particular topic. Let the menu become the framework for capturing and categorizing all of the ideas that are advanced in the discussion. In this way, the PLC team can see the entire scope of ideas and, at the same time, get a sense of the time and effort needed to actually implement them. The metaphor also provides an opportunity for some creative thinking about the various services that PLCs can offer students to ensure their success in school.

Elaboration (How to use it!)

Possible pivot points for the Menu of Ideas: homework help, test prep, class projects, independent work, contracts, instructional issues, attendance and tardiness, discipline options, or comprehending informational text.

Comprehending Informational Text		
Appetizers	*The Meal*	*Desserts*
Vocabulary cards	Summarizing exercises	Visualization strategies

MORPH GRID III: LEADING PLCs

Captivate Strategy 6. Mediated Journal Entry

Explanation (What it is!)

A *Mediated Journal Entry* is an advance organizer in which the page headings are pre-determined or guided by the leader. To use this idea in the PLC, the pages of a fold-over paper journal are labeled to include the items that will come under discussion during the session, or over the next several sessions.

Example: Mediated Journal Entry on Student Achievement Data

Cover—Data! Dialogue! Decisions!

Page 1—What . . . data?

Page 2—So what . . . does data imply?

Page 3—Now, what . . . do we do?

Page 4—What else? Who will do what, when?

As the session unfolds, PLC members record key ideas on the appropriate pages. They will keep the journal until the topic is concluded and all of the pages have been addressed.

Application (When to use it!)

The Mediated Journal can be used anytime throughout the work of the PLC. It provides a place to capture key ideas and to keep them handy, at a glance if you will, for the next meeting. It is usually helpful if the scope of the Mediated Journal encompasses one topic. Then, an entirely new Mediated Journal can be organized for a subsequent topic.

By referring to the journal throughout the meeting and capturing the notes and ideas as the discussion proceeds, the team members remain more attentive to and engaged in the issues. The Mediated Journal is also worth its weight in gold as a record of the PLC team meetings. That is sometimes a requirement for the PLCs as they progress.

Elaboration (How to use it!)

How about a PLC Getting Started Mediated Journal?

1. PLC members' e-mail or cell phone number
2. PLC Protocols (start on time, rotating leadership . . .)
3. PLC Statement of Purpose
4. PLC Pending Topics
5. PLC Key Data
6. PLC SMART Goal
7. PLC Intervention Strategies
8. PLC Results

MORPH GRID III: LEADING PLCs

Captivate Strategy 7. TAGI—That's a Good Idea!

Explanation (What it is!)

TAGI—That's a Good Idea! is a discussion strategy. It is a response stem that dictates a positive look at the idea. "That's a good idea because . . . " requires that the listener finds aspects of value in the idea being presented. Sometimes that positive remark is all that is needed to develop a fledging idea into a worthy goal. This response strategy is often a little hard in the beginning, but like a number of other strategies talked about in this book, once team members use this positive feedback strategy over several meetings, it becomes a norm for the group.

Application (When to use it!)

Sometimes PLCs fall into the chummy habit of "put-downs." It is part of the back and forth of the team members. Put-downs are cynical ways to make fun of an idea: "That's not that bright," "I can't believe you said that," or "Only you could dream that one up."

To get beyond the sarcasm of fellow faculty members, the strategy of That's a Good Idea! works every time. It really is useful during brainstorming sessions. When the team is trying to think of topics to pursue or when they are generating intervention strategies or data facts and stats, the strategy of That's a Good Idea! is ideal. It keeps the focus on positive thinking, and it guarantees a problem-solving mode.

Elaboration (How to use it!)

For example, when one member says, "I think we, as the teaching team, need to identify the kids we think are in need of help, regardless of what the test scores say," the next speaker says, "That's a good idea because we really know these kids. We see them in everyday situations. It is more like running film footage than viewing a point in time photograph."

Another example is about an intervention for increasing comprehension skills with middle-level students. One teacher says, "I have an effective strategy that I use with some of my struggling readers. It involves paired reading and discussions using a directed reading and thinking activity. It seems to get good results, and even better, it gets fast results that are visible." The next team member responds, "I think that is a good idea because if we can get some fast results in a positive direction, we will know we are on the right track. Let's try it for a few weeks and see what happens."

MORPH GRID III: LEADING PLCs

Captivate Strategy 8. Card Storming

Explanation (What it is!)

Card Storming is a group activity that provides fodder for a robust discussion of issues in which all team members participate. First and foremost, the leader announces the topic. Then, there are three basic steps or phases to the process:

1. Brainstorm a bunch of brainy ideas

2. Create commonsense clusters

3. Look at and log a larger label

More specifically, (1) individual members put personal comments or ideas about the topic on sticky notes, using a few words; (2) in turn, members place the notes into "commonsense clusters" on a large board; (3) then, the entire group decides on an all-encompassing, "generalizable" label for the various clusters.

This process allows the major concerns to surface in a way that includes everyone's ideas. As the conversation revolves around the meanings of the various clusters, a depth of understanding occurs. This discussion moves forward with clarification as ideas crystallize.

Application (When to use it!)

This is a particularly good strategy to use when there is a topic that has already generated concern among the members. It allows all ideas, no matter how different, to find voice on the display board. It also works well, once the teams are familiar with the strategy, to unpack team members' ideas quickly and without discrimination. Every idea gets an equal amount of time and space on the display. It also gives everyone a bird's eye view of the depth and breadth of the concerns and issues that emerge.

Elaboration (How to use it!)

A PLC leader who placed the topic "Hard Data versus Soft Data" on the board illustrated an example of a Card Sort. Members wrote out three to five cards or sticky notes and then were asked to put them up on the display and talk briefly about the card and about why it was sorted into one of the clusters then labeled by the team. The board looked like this as the discussion began:

Qualitative Data	Quantitative Data
Anecdotal	Test scores
Stories	Grades and GPAs
Portfolios	Report cards

MORPH GRID III: LEADING PLCs

Captivate Strategy 9. Double Entry Journal

Explanation (What it is!)

The *Double Entry Journal* is a journal format that allows a dual purpose. It provides for two entries, just as the name says. Enter a description of what occurred, and then enter a reflection about what occurred. The first entry is often a delineation of the actions under scrutiny, while the second entry is a look back and an evaluation of sorts about those actions. It truly provides for a robust entry as the teacher or team member reviews the activity and then thinks about how it went. It taps into cognitive and metacognitive thinking at the same time.

Application (When to use it!)

With the Double Entry Journal, the two entries can be made at the same time, but more often than not, the reflection is entered a bit later. This allows more time for the results to be revealed. These journals can be used in the midst of the work that the PLC is doing to revisit the actions and reflect on the progress.

Elaboration (How to use it!)

Student Attendance	
DESCRIPTION	REFLECTION
We reviewed attendance records for our group of ninth-grade students over the last two years.	As we reviewed the attendance records of our students, we noticed a change from early in the first year of seventh grade until late in the eighth-grade year.
We charted the information on graphs for each student showing the span of the 24 months.	We noticed a dramatic increase in female absenteeism as the end of eighth grade drew closer.
Then, we analyzed the graphs, trying to capture several key elements: time of year, gender, patterns, and surprises.	Now, we are trying to find out why. Maybe we can do a survey of the girls and get some information that way.

MORPH GRID III: LEADING PLCs

Captivate Strategy 10. Micro-Book Study

Explanation (What it is!)

A *Micro-Book Study* is an informative activity in which group members agree to read the same book over a designated period of time and use the readings as a pivot point for follow-up discussions. In short, the book study protocols involve three phases:

1. *Selecting* a particular book, an agreed upon schedule for the reading, and a leader to direct the discussion of the essential questions for each section.

2. *Collecting* ideas as you read and noting responses for later discussion and debriefing.

3. *Reflecting* on the responses of the others during a PLC book study meeting time as the discussion unfolds, and relating it to your work.

Please reference RFA's *The Perfect Book Study* (click the Ideas tab at www.robinfogarty.com), for more detailed instructions and illustrations of this PLC Micro-Book Study process.

Application (When to use it!)

Many PLCs begin their work as an official group with a focused book study. It is a nonthreatening way to begin professional conversations with colleagues. It is also an appropriate activity for the PLC as they enter into a new area of focus. For example, if the PLC is addressing the idea of common assessments, a book on formative assessments, the new In a Nutshell Book, *InFormative Assessments: When It's Not About a Grade,* by Fogarty and Kerns (2009), might provide the informative input needed to get started.

Elaboration (How to use it!)

One example of PLCs using book studies can be seen in the Idaho Falls school district. The principals and the staff development team selected a book, *Close the Achievement Gap: Simple Strategies That Work,* by Pete and Fogarty (2005a), for district-wide distribution to all staff. Then, each school within the district created PLC book study teams that made sense to them. Some did grade-level teams or department teams or core academic teams. Each team decided how they would study the book. Ideas ranged from discussion questions to role plays, from strategy sessions to partner debriefings.

MORPH GRID III: LEADING PLCs

Captivate Strategy 11. The Three-Story Intellect

Explanation (What it is!)

The Three-Story Intellect is a statement that reflects the concept of higher-order thinking for students and for teachers. Extrapolated from Oliver Wendell Holmes' book, *The Poet at the Breakfast-Table,* it provides a concise rendition of higher levels of thinking.

The Three-Story Intellect

There are one-story intellects,

Two story intellects and

Three story intellects with skylights.

All fact collectors who have no aim

Beyond their facts are one-story [minds].

Two-story [minds] compare, reason, and generalize,

Using the labors of the fact collectors as their own.

Three-story [minds] idealize, imagine, and predict

Their best illumination comes from above,

Through the skylight.

Application (When to use it!)

Used as a guide for robust and rich PLC discussions, The Three-Story Intellect becomes a natural strategy to bridge directly into classroom instruction. The three levels are easier to handle than the six levels of Bloom's taxonomy, yet the concept of questioning levels driving good thinking is kept intact. It simplifies the concept of questioning levels.

Elaboration (How to use it!)

One use of the Three-Story Intellect in a PLC session was focused on parent involvement. Utilizing it to think through the focus issues, the PLC leader structured the following three levels of thinking: gathering the facts, comparing the pros and cons, and illuminating alternative solutions.

Facts: Many parents aren't involved; some are scared of coming to school.

Comparing: More are involved when the kids perform; some will never come.

Alternative Solutions: Let's have kids involved in some way; think of options.

MORPH GRID III: LEADING PLCs

Captivate Strategy 12. Fat and Skinny Questions

Explanation (What it is!)

Fat and Skinny Questions are different kinds of questions that permeate classroom interactions. To make PLC members more aware of the question levels that are targeted in the classroom, these Fat and Skinny Questions can also be used in staff room activities. This gives everyone practice using the different types of questions and becoming more skillful in determining when and how to use the higher-order questions to access student thinking.

Application (When to use it!)

Everything done in the PLC sessions should promote student learning and increased achievement for all youngsters. That is the overarching purpose of all Professional Learning Communities. PLC sessions offer the perfect place to raise teacher awareness and to encourage the use of rich, robust, and rigorous questions in the classroom. Simply post the following little ditty about Fat and Skinny Questions. Use this information as a check for the kinds of questions asked and answered in the PLC sessions. It makes everyone aware of upping the ante with divergent, open-ended questions in the classroom.

Elaboration (How to use it!)

Fat and Skinny Questions

Divergent, or Fat, Questions:
   Fat questions are divergent in nature. They require discussions, examples, illustrations, clarifications, and delineations to respond fully.

Fat questions:	How would we describe that?
	Why would we want to do that?
	How might we utilize this information?

Convergent, or Skinny, Questions:
   Skinny questions are convergent questions, dead ends. There is no real thinking necessary to respond. Skinny questions require simple responses: "yes," "no," or "maybe so."

Skinny questions:	Do we all agree?
	Do you want to continue?
	Will you take this responsibility?

MORPH GRID III: LEADING PLCs

Close Strategy 1. What? So What? Now What?

Explanation (What it is!)

These three questions, *What? So what? Now what?* survey the territory for a full and comprehensive response. They require a descriptive answer that helps to process information or to reflect. The questions used, following an interaction, become a summarizing piece.

What is the gist?

So what does it mean?

Now, what should we do?

Application (When to use it!)

Often used as a set of three, What? So what? Now what? are perfect questions to sum up the work, as mentioned here. The questions can work especially well after a team task as a way to reexamine the key points discussed and decided upon. Yet they also work as an analysis tool during the actual work of the PLC. Used in this way, the three questions actually guide the work and act as a catalyst to move the thinking from one point to the next.

Elaboration (How to use it!)

One well-utilized application of the What? So what? Now what? questions is with data discussion. In fact, having members respond to these three questions is highly effective when the PLC focus is on examining student data. In a simplified example, it looks something like this:

Middle School Discipline Data	
What data do we have?	Answer: 400 more discipline referrals this year
So what does that mean?	Answer: Whatever we are doing is not working well
Now, what will we do?	Answer: Let's brainstorm some ideas

Without elaborating, it is possible to see using these questions to structure the data discussions for the PLC. It truly does keep the talk on track.

MORPH GRID III: LEADING PLCs

Close Strategy 2. Signals—Red/Yellow/Green

Explanation (What it is!)

The use of classroom signals is as old as the hills. It is a strategy that skillful teachers use to engage students in the learning by maximizing the feedback from them. Yet this strategy also works to structure the PLC discussions so they are more constructively interactive. Teachers use three colors of sticky notes

Red means "Stop! I'm not sure I agree; I feel some dissonance."

Yellow means "Slow down! May I paraphrase, clarify, or illustrate."

Green means "Keep going. I'm with you; I see this working; right on."

Application (When to use it!)

This strategy may seem a bit hokey at first for adult learners, but trust in the process of group work. As the PLC matures, the members sometimes fall into a groove. The same people ask the questions, the same people voice their opinions when it comes to decisions, and the same people assume informal leadership roles that make the group a functioning PLC. Yet others may want to or need to step up to the plate and assume more responsibility than they have up to a certain point. These kinds of tools—the red, yellow, and green signals—help to break down the routines that have been established.

Of course, using it in the staff setting of PLCs reminds teachers of its value in getting everyone involved. They will take it back to their class discussions, with highly visible and highly positive results with the students.

Elaboration (How to use it!)

The *Signals—Red/Yellow/Green* strategy was used in a PLC to guide a critical discussion in a middle school about whether or not to retain the Core Team concept of having language arts, math, science, and social studies teachers on a team, or whether to change to a departmental approach.

RED—"Wait a minute. Let's not rush to judgment on the Core Team."

YELLOW—"I need to clarify how the departmental teams would work."

GREEN—"Yes, this is making sense in light of our increasing population."

The strategy worked so well in keeping the discussion professional and positive that it sparked an idea for one PLC: They decided that at every PLC meeting they would pledge to employ an interactive classroom strategy.

MORPH GRID III: LEADING PLCs

Close Strategy 3. Five Minutes of Metacognition

Explanation (What it is!)

Five Minutes of Metacognition is a reflection strategy between A and B partners. When the partners meet, they take turns commenting reflectively on the issues following this structured schedule of interaction.

Partner A: 2 minutes to state immediate reaction

Partner B: 2 minutes to state immediate reaction

Partner A: 30 seconds to summarize final thoughts

Partner B: 30 seconds to summarize final thoughts

It is a simple way to ensure that both people get a chance to reflect and that they are listening and responding to what the other said. While two minutes does not seem like much time, it really is enough time for each of the PLC members to develop and promote a thought and to summarize a final thought based on both respondents' thinking.

Application (When to use it!)

Use this to summarize, as suggested by the *closing strategy* label given. But also use this to open the next meeting. The Five Minutes of Metacognition is effective as a reboot strategy. It helps target the thinking from the previous meeting because members try to share a reflection about the progress made and the key issues discussed. It also has great possibilities for the classroom, as do all of these strategies. In addition, the structure is time-bound so it works nicely with tight schedules and an overloaded curriculum.

Elaboration (How to use it!)

A great example of Five Minutes of Metacognition was illustrated by a PLC leader who adopted this strategy. He used it to talk about their session on the excessive use and persistent evidence of plagiarism with the students. He asked the teachers on the team to pair up and reflect on the discussion they had had using this structured model of reflection.

Partner A: It is far more pervasive than I realized . . . it was enlightening to hear all the varied examples of how kids do this . . . (2 minutes)

Partner B: Really. They are pretty darn creative with their plagiarisms . . . what a range of innovative disguises they attempt . . . (2 minutes)

Partner A: My early conclusion is . . . (30 seconds)

Partner B: Maybe, but I'm thinking that if we . . . (30 seconds)

MORPH GRID III: LEADING PLCs

Close Strategy 4. On a Scale of 1 to 10! Justify!

Explanation (What it is!)

This is a team evaluation tool that helps members reveal their thinking on the issue or on the work of the PLC in that session. Team members rank the idea under scrutiny at the time. "On a scale of 1 to 10, I give this idea a(n) ___." Or they might say, "On a scale of 1 to 10, I give our work today a(n) ___ because ___."

Then, they continue with a justification for their ranking. By going around the group and allowing each person to weigh in, the team has a better idea of what everyone is thinking regarding the idea. This is a more authentic reading of the group opinion and support than just hearing a voice or two comment on the issue.

Application (When to use it!)

This is a nice closing strategy because it requires a summative judgment at that moment. It forces a rating and subsequent justification. When this is used on a regular basis, it creates a sense of urgency. The team members realize that they are really working to make a difference and that the conversations they have matter. By requiring each person to rate the group ideas or the actual work and progress of the group, the PLC continues to grow into a more sophisticated working team.

Elaboration (How to use it!)

"On a scale of 1 to 10, how would you rate our choice of books this term for the book studies?" was the question posed by one PLC leader as the term was coming to an end.

"I rate it a 7 because I like the choices, but the time to digest them was too short."

"I think I would rate it a 9 because I know I never would have read the books on my own, and I learned a lot."

"For me, I guess I would say a 5. I might have picked books more in my discipline."

"I was pretty happy with the talks that resulted. I also give it a 9."

"Can I give it a 9.5? I really, really benefited from the book studies."

MORPH GRID III: LEADING PLCs

Close Strategy 5. E-mail/Text Buddies' Commitment

Explanation (What it is!)

Creating text or e-mail buddies from the PLC members is a powerful communication tool for the PLC. It is sometimes difficult to have real-time conversations during the busy schedule of the typical school day. A short text message or e-mail is a powerful tech tool for keeping in touch. It's an expedient method of sending out an idea that occurs to a member following a session. If she or he waited until the next meeting, it might never get shared. By putting it out there in an informal way, one allows others to piggyback on it or at least think about it before the next meeting.

Application (When to use it!)

Anytime! Just about anywhere! Texts or e-mails are the name of the game. Texting and e-mailing provide a ready communication tool that is used effectively around the PLC sessions. Members can check in with questions before they meet and follow up with comments that occur to them after the session is over. There really is nothing like these quick, effortless, and handy tech tools for continuing the conversations.

Elaboration (How to use it!)

One leader of a PLC suggested that the members commit to sending one e-mail or text to other members between every meeting. They were to use it to reflect on their work or make suggestions for the next session.

He felt it would give everyone a chance to think about things away from the front-line action. In turn, he noted that it would foster deeper understanding of the issues because it does not all have to happen in the briefness and urgency of the actual PLC session.

Several texts or e-mails following a heated session on the real purpose of the PLC:

"I agree! PLC discussions must be more student-centered. But we need to vent, too!"

"BTW, u r not the only 1. I 2 want more student talk."

"Gotcha! K! Talk later!"

MORPH GRID III: LEADING PLCs

Close Strategy 6. High-Five Partner Walk/Music Stopper

Explanation (What it is!)

A *High-Five Partner Walk* is a movement activity that helps the team to change partners, change the energy, and change the dynamics of the discussion. To do the High-Five Partner Walk, teachers walk around the room and high-five everyone they pass, saying, "Hi! Five!" They keep moving until the music stops, even if they high-five the same people twice. The two people nearest each other when the music stops become High-Five Partners. That is when the leader announces the topic and the partners dialogue about the assigned topic.

Application (When to use it!)

This activity is fun with the PLC groups anytime throughout the PLC meeting. It brings a moment of music into the room and provides an opportunity for members to talk with people other than the usual suspects, and it provides freshness to the situation.

Of course, it is a marvelous closure activity, too. It helps to punctuate the end with a bit of music and movement. Everyone feels a lift of energy and the conversations are lively and insightful.

Elaboration (How to use it!)

One PLC leader used the High-Five Partner Walk/Music Stopper to mix and match the team dialogue on a "sticky wicket" issue. The debate about meeting every week for an hour had become an ongoing issue that came up at every meeting. While time is set aside in the schedule for this weekly hour meeting for all teams, some wanted to change it to a half an hour because they felt they needed the extra time for planning. Others were adamant that the hour was a regulation and they did not have control over the decision to shorten the time.

By doing the High-Five Partner Walk/Music Stopper, new partners were suddenly facing each other and new voices emerged as everyone examined the issue. After hearing the music and walking around, smiling and laughing, the conversations certainly took on a more friendly and amicable tone.

MORPH GRID III: LEADING PLCs

Close Strategy 7. Points of the Compass

Explanation (What it is!)

Points of the Compass is a management tool for moving team members into a discussion group. By using the points of the compass as a visual metaphor for four chairs together, away from the tables, members are encouraged to stay away from all of their stuff at the tables. Theory has it that this is a more conducive arrangement for dialogue and discussion. This is what is referred to as a "head to head, eye to eye, knee to knee collaborative grouping."

The leader asks the teachers in the session to form groups of four (it also works with three partners). Once the groups are formed, they take four (or three) chairs and place them as the four points of the compass. Next, the people in the four chairs are responsible for four shares. It becomes a simple round robin discussion, but it is enhanced by the proximity of the team.

Application (When to use it!)

This can be used as a final articulation to bring things to closure. It creates an atmosphere of concentration and focus as the four team members take turns discussing the ideas that had been presented earlier. It gets people looking directly at each other and that seems to be conducive to a relevant and revealing discussion. There is an intimacy in the group that provides a safety net. Teachers seem to feel more comfortable talking candidly in these small and structured settings.

Elaboration (How to use it!)

A notable use of Points of the Compass occurred when a PLC leader organized the group into the "compass chairs configuration" and asked them to read a synopsis of an article on the adolescent brain. It was a short, one-page piece that talked about three parts of the teen brain that are still developing. It also had a diagram that pointed to the areas of the brain under discussion. Short, sweet, and to the point, it was the perfect piece to use with a Points of the Compass discussion strategy.

First, the team members read the article, and then they rotated around the points of the compass as each person commented on the article. This is an effective strategy to try in the PLC setting. It changes up the usual setting.

MORPH GRID III: LEADING PLCs

Close Strategy 8. Nursery Rhyme Summary

Explanation (What it is!)

The *Nursery Rhyme Summary* is a summarizing strategy to help bring closure to ideas under discussion. In this strategy, the team uses a nursery rhyme as the framework for making summary points. Here is an example of a PLC summary about the issue of transfer of skill and drill activities to math problem solving. They summarized the idea that they cannot just assume that the kids will apply skills appropriately to the story problem, as the nursery rhyme implies. It is not "leave them alone and they will come home" . . . this is not how it works.

Little Bo Peep has lost her sheep

And doesn't know were to find them.

Leave them alone and they'll come home

Wagging their tails behind them.

After playing with this idea through the nursery rhyme, teachers perhaps will find that they have taken this idea for granted. The team settles in on what they need to change if they are to get more transfer.

Application (When to use it!)

It's sometimes a fun and efficient closure to use a specific strategy to summarize the telling points of an issue. It causes a more mindful and creative approach to finding the gist of the issue and presenting the information in a usual way.

Elaboration (How to use it!)

For example, when summarizing the data showing a deficit in problem-solving skills in third-grade math, the PLC team might create this summary of the information:

Jack and Jill went up the Problem Solving Hill

To fetch winning third grade math scores.

Jack and the boys fell down on story problems,

And Jill and the girls tumbled along a little better.

While it sounds a little silly, this kind of activity requires all the PLC members to join in to make a summary statement that depicts the data as accurately as possible, although in a nutshell. This little nursery rhyme makes the point that the boys may need more or different interventions than the girls.

MORPH GRID III: LEADING PLCs

Close Strategy 9. Letter Journal Entry

Explanation (What it is!)

Journaling is a reflection strategy that some PLCs choose to use as their work unfolds. It is a powerful technique that can be used to look back on the discussions and decisions made in the sessions or to project forward thoughts and concerns about ideas that are pending. Using the *Letter Journal Entry* provides a format that is quite open-ended and easy-flowing.

To write a reflection in the form of a letter changes the tone and the tenor of the writing. As the PLC leader, suggest that teachers can address issues discussed or ideas under consideration in the letter to another teacher, a parent, the principal, a mentor or coach, or even their spouse. Just have them begin, "Dear ____," and see what happens. Then, remind them that they will be sharing them next time, so there is some understanding of accountability. (Naturally, the leader always gives the option to pass when asking for sharing on journal entries.)

Application (When to use it!)

Use this strategy as a summary piece at the end of a PLC meeting. Bring the journals in to the next meeting and read them as a starting point for the unfinished business from the former session. Or use them in the session and write about a topic that is under study. Just like many other interactive and reflective strategies mentioned in this chapter, the reflection through a letter journal format is surprisingly helpful to PLC work. It is one of those ideas that the PLC has to try before they understand the power of these structured tools. Yet we do know that PLCs that use various structures in their sessions tend to function well.

Elaboration (How to use it!)

An example of a Letter Journal Entry illustrates the clarity that it can provide as the team members unpack their thinking about an issue of concern. One PLC leader gave these instructions: "Write a Letter Journal Entry about our difficult discussion on dropout rates and how we, as a school, can be more encouraging to students about staying in school."

Dear Dr. Smuthers,

As a student in graduate school, my focus was aligned to yours—middle-level education. We are now struggling with an increasing concern about the rising drop out rate with our ninth graders. As our "at-risk" kids enter high school, start earning some money, and get a taste of that perceived freedom, they opt to leave school behind and enter into the world of work. We are brainstorming ideas to reverse this disturbing trend. What can we do?

MORPH GRID III: LEADING PLCs

Close Strategy 10. Q & A

Explanation (What it is!)

The *Q & A* is a Question and Answer structure that is often part of other discussion strategies. It is sometimes the most powerful part of the PLC meeting. Q & As are structured in several different ways. The group can post questions and the responses can be handled by the leader or with random responses from the group members. It can also be helpful to keep a record of FAQs (Frequently Asked Questions) for future reference and clarification. This is how PLCs become more effective and skillful over time.

Another way to orchestrate a Q & A is to select a panel of several members and have them prepare to respond to questions on the issue of concern. In this way, some members take responsibility for doing some extra research. Thus, the PLC has the advantage of more informed responses.

Application (When to use it!)

To begin or end the PLC session with a question and answer segment often illuminates the real concerns and issues on the minds of the PLC team members. It is the time when everyone gets to ask questions that may have been nagging at them or when they actually raise questions that have occurred in the sessions but have never been satisfactorily answered.

Elaboration (How to use it!)

A PLC Q & A strategy in a rural elementary school asked members to post their questions on the Response to Intervention (RTI) initiative that is on the agenda for the next school year. A Q & A summary is shown here:

1. QUESTION: What is considered quality instruction for Tier 1?

   ANSWER: Active, engaged, multimodal instruction is the basics of . . .

2. QUESTION: Is Reciprocal Teaching a Tier 1 or a Tier 2 strategy?

   ANSWER: It could be either, depending on our overall plan . . .

3. QUESTION: Is Tier 3 Special Education services?

   ANSWER: Not necessarily. It is also classroom-based . . . Regular Ed strategies are . . .

4. QUESTION: How and when do we screen all students?

   ANSWER: We will screen all students early in the year with . . . And then monitor progress . . .

5. QUESTION: Aren't we already doing tiered instruction with differentiation?

   ANSWER: Yes, in a way. However, tiered instructional planning is data driven . . .

MORPH GRID III: LEADING PLCs

Close Strategy 11. Bridging Snapshots/Visual Metaphor

Explanation (What it is!)

Bridging Snapshots /Visual Metaphor is a reflection strategy that illuminates understanding. To do this strategy, the PLC leader has the group brainstorm 15 to 20 "snapshots" of the meeting issues on chart paper. Then the members "bridge" these isolated snapshots through discussions by drawing connecting lines to show how they are connected to each other. This is how the issues are analyzed and clarified.

Finally, the team synthesizes the entire discussion by finding and developing a visual metaphor. This means that they will draw a concrete object (balloons, flowers, tombstones, or even a chair), a scene (skyline, tree-lined lane, or train on a track), or a symbol (the yin and the yang, a *no* symbol, or a circle graphic) that depicts the essence of the conversation. They will work together to find a metaphor that works, and then they will illustrate it on a poster paper.

Application (When to use it!)

Use this as a grand closing to a topic that has been under study for some time and is coming to a close. It takes a little time, but it has such effective applications to the classroom that it is worth working through one as a PLC and modeling the power of this summary tool. Once the snapshots are out, the visual metaphor will unfold in all its glory as the team gets to work. In turn, it will illuminate many of the key points of the discussion.

Elaboration (How to use it!)

Example Topic: Grading Practices

Snapshots:

Inconsistencies, frequency, validity, reliability, parent issues, student competition, electronic records of grades, green grade book, letter grades, averaging, giving zeroes, weighting, purposes, unfinished work, poor quality work, rightness and correctness and accuracy, precision in work, pride in completed work...

Visual Metaphor:

Imagine the scales of justice or a barbell weight as a metaphor to depict the issues that surfaced around the topic of grading practices.

Barbell of Balance: hard and soft data

MORPH GRID III: LEADING PLCs

Close Strategy 12. Panel of Experts

Explanation (What it is!)

The *Panel of Experts* is a discussion tool that really animates the topic and the members participating in this PLC activity. There is nothing more powerful than creating a Panel of Experts to expose the issues in a lively debate. To use this activity in the PLC, the members work in teams of two. One is the expert, and the other is his or her agent or manager. Each team is assigned an expert point of view around the target issue. Then, in pairs, the teams prepare questions and responses to represent their point of view. Finally, they come to the panel (in costume, with props, if willing . . . even a hat works to transform) ready to debate. The leader acts as the moderator and keeps the debate for the Panel of Experts flowing.

Application (When to use it!)

Use this when the PLC is researching an issue of concern. It spreads the research out to the various members in a jigsaw of sorts. The experts on the panel represent the varying viewpoints. While this activity does take time and preparation for the PLC, it represents a lifelong skill for adult learning because it requires research and presentation skills. Of course, it is not something that PLCs do every day. It is a robust approach to examining an issue from all perspectives. Try it and see. It is worth the time and energy it takes because the presentations are usually unforgettable.

Elaboration (How to use it!)

Example Issue: The Data-Driven Classroom

Panel of Experts represented:

Mike Schmoker, Doug Reeves, Kati Haycock, Robert Marzano, Rick Stiggins, Dylan Wiliam, James Popham. (Check the Web for information on their positions.)

Each team must research the various points and be ready to argue and debate with the others. Just try it! It truly is a remarkable learning scenario for the PLC members who become immersed in the issues. And, of course, it works like a dream in the classroom, too.

4

Morph Grid IV

Facilitating Group Work

Whole Group	Small Group	Individual
1. 2-4-8 Focus Interview (page 121)	1. TTYPA . . . (page 135)	1. One-Minute Write (page 147)
2. Inside/Outside Circles (page 122)	2. The Three Musketeers (page 136)	2. Mediated Journal Entry (page 148)
3. Human Graph/Take a Stand (page 123)	3. ABC Graffiti (page 137)	3. Goal Setting (page 149)
4. Yellow Brick Road (page 125)	4. Four-Fold Concept Development (page 138)	4. Mr. Parnes' Questions (page 150)
5. Magic Book (page 126)	5. Cooperative Learning Tear Share (page 139)	5. Letter of Commitment (page 151)
6. The Tiny Transfer Book (page 128)	6. Jigsaw/Expert Jigsaw (page 140)	6. Mrs. Potter's Questions (page 152)
7. Energizers/Hurrahs/ Cheers (page 129)	7. Pyramid Game (page 141)	7. Reflective Journals (page 153)
8. People Search (page 130)	8. AB Partners (page 142)	8. Ms. Poindexter's Questions (page 154)
9. Carousel (page 131)	9. Think Pair Share (page 143)	9. Personal Experience (page 155)
10. Gallery Walk (page 132)	10. High-Five Walk (page 144)	10. PMI—Plus! Minus! Interesting! (page 156)
11. Birthday Line Up (page 133)	11. 3-2-1 Connect (page 145)	11. Parking Lot (page 157)
12. Puzzle Building (page 134)	12. Dial Information 4-1-1 (page 146)	12. Highlights/Insights (page 158)

INTRODUCTION

Facilitating group work requires skill and great talent. There are many occasions when a facilitator saves the day by utilizing the just-in-time activity to make the session a productive one. Whether it be an individual endeavor, or a small grade-level team, a core middle school team, a departmental team, an entire faculty, or even several school staffs gathered together, the skillful facilitator knows how to structure the day for success.

From Staff Room to Classroom II: The One-Minute Professional Development Planner presents a treasure trove of strategies for small and whole group interactions. From easy-to-do cooperative activities for two or three learners grouped together to total room interactions that structure activity for the entire group, the ideas are here to try.

DIRECTIONS

Roll a set of dice three times to select an activity for the three elements based on the numbers rolled. Be courageous and go with the actual numbers. Don't cheat. It will make your facilitation of group work lively, original, and effective as you integrate large group, small group, and individual activities in the session.

1. Whole group

2. Small group

3. Individual endeavor

CATEGORICAL LISTING OF ALL MORPH TOOLS

Check Appendix A for an index of strategies by type of tool (e.g., collaborative tool or management tool).

CREATIVE OPTIONS

Remember, the strategies work in any order. An opener may be a small or large group activity, or even an individual activity. Likewise, the middle of the session and the end of the session have the same flexibility. Be creative and use the grid of strategies with your own creative flair.

MORPH GRID IV: FACILITATING GROUP WORK

Whole Group Strategy 1. 2-4-8 Focus Interview

Explanation (What it is!)

This is a dynamic way to involve a large group of people in a very engaging strategy that demonstrates the difference between engaged and active learning. While it is executed best with a personal artifact from their pocket or purse, so that everyone has something unique in his or her hands, it can also be done without an object.

Two (2)—A and B partners share book reports, essays, show and tell items, or even lab logs. They take turns showing the artifact and telling about it in some detail. Each partner actively and attentively listens to the other. The first interaction is 3 minutes long, with 90 seconds for each to speak. When finished, they find another set of A and B partners.

Four (4)—Each of the partners takes the first partner's artifact and tells the partner's story, rather than his or her own. Again, the foursome takes turns telling each other's stories and then moves toward another group of four, to make a group of eight. Instead of 90 seconds, each person has to tell their partner's story in 60 seconds—4 people with 60 seconds each, 4 minutes of talking.

Eight (8)—The group of A and B partners finds another group of A and B partners. This time, each person in the group must tell a third story by holding the artifact of the other person and using it to tell that story. Each person has 30 seconds to tell his or her partner's story—8 stories, 30 seconds each, is 4 minutes of talking.

Application (When to use it!)

The purpose of this exercise is to encourage and facilitate active, attentive listening, as well as full participation by each member. Notice that as the groups become larger, it becomes quieter in the room because only a few people are talking at a time. It is a sound listening strategy to practice as a skillful facilitator, even if you only do a 2-4 grouping, because it does create a "focus interview" scenario that requires good listening. The 2-4-8 can be used to uncover prior knowledge or as a review.

Elaboration (How to use it!)

At a 90-minute conference session on classroom management, where the speaker wanted to emphasize active learning as a vital part of a well-managed classroom, begin with a 2-4-8 Focus Interview. The story that each participant is to tell is one surefire way that workflow can be managed. About 70 to 80 people stand and form pairs and begin talking. The presenter, using a pre-arranged timer, signals the pairs to move on time. Soon, the loud talking quiets as the pairs find another pair, and then on the next signal there are groups of eight, shoulder to shoulder, talking with quiet voices and with all members of the group listening intently.

MORPH GRID IV: FACILITATING GROUP WORK

Whole Group Strategy 2. Inside/Outside Circles

Explanation (What it is!)

The purpose of *Inside/Outside Circles* is to facilitate quick interactions with several different partners. It is a highly active and lively strategy, as well as a highly interactive one. Create two circles, one inside the other, with the same number of people in each circle. Instruct the inside circle to move clockwise and the outside circle to move counterclockwise. Explain that the movement will begin and end with a familiar song that they will all sing (For example, "Twinkle, Twinkle Little Star," "The Farmer in the Dell," "Ring Around the Rosy," or "Row, Row, Row Your Boat"). Then, announce the topic for discussion (e.g., challenging students, best lessons, differentiation strategies) when they stop and face a partner. Proceed with the singing and the movement. When the song ends, have them stop and face a partner from the other circle and share their stories. Repeat the interaction one or two more times, sharing with different partners each time.

Application (When to use it!)

This strategy models three aspects of effective staff development—movement; relevant, collegial conversations; and obvious applications for the classroom. We can't underestimate the energizing power of movement when teaching the adult learner; combining the singing really adds to the overall mood. When the song ends and people turn and face their new partners, there is an authentic emotional change in the group. The conversations often become so engaging and intense that participants barely notice the pairs on either side of them, which are just as actively engaged. Also, teachers can easily see ways to transfer the Inside/Outside Circle activity to the classroom. Possible interactions to facilitate include having artifacts that you want attendees to share with their Inside/Outside partner.

Elaboration (How to use it!)

An effective way to begin any professional development is to have participants share examples of their prior knowledge about the day's topic. For example, a workshop on reading strategies could begin with the Inside/Outside Circle, and when the song ends, participants could turn to their partner and talk about strategies they use to help struggling readers. Or at the end of the day, after the presenter has set clear expectations for transfer of the many new strategies that the participants have learned, end the day with the Inside/Outside Circle and have participants share one idea that they will take with them back to their classroom.

MORPH GRID IV: FACILITATING GROUP WORK

Whole Group Strategy 3. Human Graph/Take a Stand

Explanation (What it is!)

Create a graph with a topic focus that sets various gradations for participants to consider.

Topic 1: About Comprehension I Know . . .

A lot	A little	I don't know what I know	Not much	Next to nothing

Topic 2: Character in The Three Musketeers I Related to the Most Was . . .

D'Artagnan	Athos	Aramis	Porthos	Lady de Winter

Topic 3: Would You Rather Be . . .

A fraction	or	A decimal

To help participants see things from other points of view—a valuable skill in persuasive writing, problem solving, and seeking consensus—begin the graph with the following question:

Topic 4: "Where Are Your Students in Terms of Comfort and Expertise With Technology?"

Techno-Wannabe	TechnoSavvy	TechnoTutor	TechnoCrat	TechnoWizard

Once you have the topic focus, have participants take a stand on the imaginary axis line of the imaginary bar graph and talk to others around them. They should tell why they selected that stance and justify their thinking about it. This activity requires decision-making and justification for the decision on the part of each participant.

After sufficient time, sample the various opinions of the whole group. Allow people to change positions if, and when, they hear something that makes them question their decision and change their minds. Also, ask questions about how quickly they made up their minds and about how decisive or how negotiable they were—it adds to the reflection about decision-making processes.

Application (When to use it!)

The *Human Graph* works as a way to discover what your audience knows about the topic of the day or to delineate what they know or think about key concepts that comprise the topic.

If used to uncover prior knowledge, the group could return to the graph at the end of the day to compare what they know now versus what they knew at the start of the day.

(Continued)

(Continued)

Elaboration (How to use it!)

Before sampling the content of the Human Graph, ask the participants to make a data statement, look at the information represented in the graph, and make an observation. Make clear that this is a great way to model for the classroom the difference between abstract, representative, and concrete information. Allow time for participants to share with those in their lines and with the whole class as each line is sampled.

MORPH GRID IV: FACILITATING GROUP WORK

Whole Group Strategy 4. Yellow Brick Road

Explanation (What it is!)

A marvelous graphing option using four corners, *Yellow Brick Road* is a way to sample prior knowledge or to appraise a learned strategy or concept. In this interaction, participants are asked to select a labeled corner of the room based on their depth of understanding about a new learning that has been introduced.

Under Construction—Still making sense of it

Rocky Road—Moving along, but some bumps in the road

Yellow Brick Road—Feeling confident about it

Highway to Heaven—Smooth ride all the way

Once participants have moved, have them chat with others in their corner and then take a reading of the numbers in each group. Finally, sample and debrief with the entire group about moving on to new information or revisiting and reviewing this information again.

Application (When to use it!)

Use this strategy when working with teachers who are in the process of implementing a new instructional initiative in order to discover their level of understanding. Allow time for participants to talk; to ensure full participation, facilitate the groups so that there are pairs talking and not one big group listening to one person speak. The Yellow Brick Road, when used as a closing activity, allows the entire audience to see how everyone feels or thinks about the topic at hand.

Possible Topics:

My comfort level with the subject of formative assessment is . . .

The states of the professional learning communities in our school are . . .

As a new teacher, my feeling about my classroom management is . . .

Elaboration (How to use it!)

Some training spaces will lend themselves to the Yellow Brick Road instead of the Human Graph simply because of the configuration of the furniture. Have everyone stand and push in their chairs to allow room to move. Allow those who can't seem find a spot that reflects what they are feeling to designate their own area of the room and label and defend their thinking. "We are on the Dirt Path; it's smoother than the Rocky Road but not quite all the way to Yellow Brick Road."

MORPH GRID IV: FACILITATING GROUP WORK

Whole Group Strategy 5. Magic Book

Explanation (What it is!)

The *Magic Book* is constructed as a whole group activity, as a tool to capture notes and key take aways from the ensuing discussion, video, or presentation of information. The glory of this strategy is that the "magic" happens as the tabs are pulled and the pages shift from a sectioned page to a full-page spread. It allows a true dichotomy of information: the analysis on the sectioned page, and the synthesis on the full-page spread. Thus, it highlights higher-order thinking because one page requires parts of the idea and the other page calls for a putting together of the ideas.

Instructions for making the foldable called the Magic Book:

1. Each person needs two single sheets of copy paper.
2. Fold the first sheet in half (hamburger style), then tear it in half.
3. Save one half and tear it in half again, making two strips of equal length and width. Save the two strips and put the half aside.
4. Take the second whole sheet of paper and fold it in half (hamburger bun style).
5. Then, fold both sides back toward the fold, creating "wings" or the letter *w* if you look at it from the end.
6. Grasp the middle section of the same piece of paper between the two wings, and mark off two spots to create thirds.
7. Now, tear the two marked spots through the fold to the mark. When you are finished, they look like three teeth.
8. Now, open the torn paper and weave the two strips through the sections on each side.
9. After the weaving is done, fold the book together with the six sections in the middle, giving it a good crease.
10. Carefully find the middle, and open to these six sections. Close it again.
11. Carefully find the two flaps beneath the six-sectioned middle, and pull those far edges out to see the big "magic" page that is hidden behind the six sections.

The Magic Book is ready for the note-taking activity. Directions for the Magic Book are also available on the RFA Web site (www.robinfogarty.com/makingthelittlebooks76.html).

Application (When to use it!)

Use the Magic Book when you have six or eight concepts and a flow chart that you want to capture using a memorable foldable that models the best practice of summarizing and note taking. The bulleted concepts go into the interior boxes, and when you pull the tabs, there is the graphic representation.

Elaboration (How to use it!)

Do not hesitate to use this strategy because you think it will take too long or that your audience will not be able to follow along. Modeling active learning strategies that teachers are expected to transfer back to the classroom is the only way to help them "get it." The adult learner wants step by step learning, so scaffold the lesson, and remember, leave no teachers behind.

MORPH GRID IV: FACILITATING GROUP WORK

Whole Group Strategy 6. The Tiny Transfer Book

Explanation (What it is!)

One of the most versatile and popular foldables is the Little Book, or what is often called *The Tiny Transfer Book,* because it is a perfect take-away tool. Simply fold one single sheet of paper (size may vary depending on the desired size of the final product). A little pocket-sized booklet is created and ready for note taking.

Directions for The Tiny Transfer Book:

1. Fold a sheet of paper in half the short way (a hamburger bun or taco fold). Then, fold it in half again, into four corners, and then fold it in half one more time. When you open the paper, it will have eight sections on it.

2. Now, fold the paper again into the hamburger bun. Keep the fold at the top and tear along the center vertical through the fold to the horizontal mark, half way down. If you did this correctly, there should be a hole in the middle of the paper that you can look through.

3. After the tear has been made, refold the paper the long way, like a hot dog bun or a burrito. The fold and the hole are on the top.

4. Hold both ends of the hotdog fold and push the ends toward the center (your hands are pushing toward each other) until all four sections touch. It looks kind of like a pinwheel.

5. Then, gently fold the pages around and you have a little book with a cover and seven pages.

6. Put the ragged edges on the bottom and you are ready to make a cover.

Directions for the Tiny Transfer Book are also available on the RFA Web site (www.robinfogarty.com/makingthelittlebooks76.html).

Application (When to use it!)

There are seven pages to The Tiny Transfer Book, not counting the cover, so it works well if you have six or seven key concepts you want your audience to remember. Double pages can be used if there are three main points plus the back cover. Three main ideas can be written across the double pages, resulting in nine spaces plus the back cover.

Elaboration (How to use it!)

Because of its smallness, it is an easy way to transport the key points you want participants to remember. The applications are endless! Tiny Transfer Books can be made with colored paper, with a different color for different days in multiple day trainings.

MORPH GRID IV: FACILITATING GROUP WORK

Whole Group Strategy 7. Energizers/Hurrahs/Cheers

Explanation (What it is!)

There is nothing like a quick *Energizer* or cheer to provide some needed movement or a shift in the energy. These are short little cheers that everyone does as the leader models the *Hurrah!* One example is the "Roller Coaster Cheer." Everyone "clicks, clicks, clicks" as they put their arms up in the air. Once they reach the highest point, they move their hands down in three dipping strokes as they say, "Whew, whew, whew!" There are many of these available, but it's also fun to make them up for certain occasions.

Application (When to use it!)

Use Energizers as a replacement to a regular round of applause whenever groups present back to the entire class. Take the time to model the Energizer, and then get everyone to follow along as they "celebrate" the team that just presented.

Also, it is important to have plenty of Energizers ready to demonstrate because it is best not to repeat any of them. When every Energizer you model is new, it reinforces the value of using new and unique strategies and ideas in the classroom.

Elaboration (How to use it!)

Always remind the reluctant participants that what the Energizer models is how much movement in the classroom is needed to increase or optimize blood flow into your brain. This is the only way that oxygen and all the important nutrients that the brain needs will reach it. When these substances do reach the brain, the mind will have a better capacity to process and store information.

Energizers affect the audience on an emotional level: excitement, fun, surprise, empathy, and even embarrassment stimulate the learner. Through their emotions, we get their attention; with their attention, we get cognition; with cognition, we get memory; and memory is the only evidence of learning.

MORPH GRID IV: FACILITATING GROUP WORK

Whole Group Strategy 8. People Search

Explanation (What it is!)

The *People Search* sends the participants out into the group with a list of statements that they use to connect with other people for a dialogue. After someone has shared with you, you get them to sign or initial your sheet as evidence of the dialogue.

The People Search also helps teachers understand the value of open-ended statements or questions. If the People Search has low-level, simple yes-or-no questions, there will be shorter interactions and participants will end up more concerned with getting the required signatures than with the depth of the topic.

Emphasize that the People Search is about the conversation, not just about completing the task.

Application (When to use it!)

Use the People Search to stir up prior knowledge and to introduce key terms or concepts that will be integral to the content of the training. For example, if conferencing skills for coaches is the topic, "Find someone who can arrange these three parts of coaching in order of importance and can justify their thinking: preconference/observation/ postconference."

The People Search is a high-energy activity and is best scheduled after the participants have been sitting for a while, right after lunch, or to increase the energy of the staff in training scheduled after school.

Elaboration (How to use it!)

For example, a People Search on *Millennials,* or the new generation, might have the following statements to spark interactions.

Find someone who

1. knows a Millennial personally and will describe a typical trait.

2. compares and contrasts Millennials to their own generation.

3. will choose a word to describe the technology skills of the Millennials and will justify their choice.

    ___ TechnoSavvy   ___ In their DNA   ___ TechnoWannabes

4. can explain why the career ambitions of a Millennial include owning their own business.

5. suggests a tactic for working with Millennials, who love collaborations.

6. demonstrates texting as a Millennial might do it.

7. can name a popular TV show, movie, song, or musical group of Millennials.

8. can explain why Millennials are also called *Gen Y* or *Nexters.*

MORPH GRID IV: FACILITATING GROUP WORK

Whole Group Strategy 9. Carousel

Explanation (What it is!)

Use a *Carousel* when you are facilitating a number of groups who are working at easels or stations about the room. After they complete their task or product, have the entire group "carousel" around to each station as that team presents their findings. The Carousel implies that the participants move about the room, stopping periodically, to hear from the various teams. It is a great movement piece, but it also gives focus to the different viewpoints presented.

Application (When to use it!)

The Carousel is a very effective way to process information after doing a whole class jigsaw. When teams are engaged in a complex cooperative task, they want to be able to share what they have done and what they have learned. To keep the energy level high, instead of having each group come up to the front of the room and present while everyone else sits and listens, use the Carousel, which has everyone standing and moving.

A nice punctuation point after each presentation is an Energizer.

Elaboration (How to use it!)

Presentations need to be short and to the point, so model the skill of summarization and make clear to the participants just what they have to share. Emphasize that some teachers avoid whole class cooperative strategies because of the time it takes to have every team share, so that by clearly defining what each team is to communicate to the others, the Carousel remains brisk and focused. Also, scaffolding what should be shared makes it very clear what key ideas other members of the class should be writing down in their notes as they carousel around the room.

MORPH GRID IV: FACILITATING GROUP WORK

Whole Group Strategy 10. Gallery Walk

Explanation (What it is!)

Unlike the Carousel, the *Gallery Walk* implies that the participants move around the room, on their own and at their own pace, to view the "gallery of work" displayed following a prior activity. The gallery might be left in place over several days if the workshops or meetings span over time. This kind of independent viewing allows viewers to focus where they choose to focus, based on their interests, much like a real gallery walk.

Application (When to use it!)

When possible, a gallery walk can be set up before lunch with the understanding that part of the lunchtime can be used to walk the gallery, or it can even be left up over a couple days so that there is time to absorb all of the information. Doing this also models how Professional Learning Communities (PLCs) might use this strategy in their schools to display what they are working on, thus encouraging a whole school to adopt a PLC attitude.

Elaboration (How to use it!)

A Gallery Walk works well when the information displayed is complex or detailed, such as with lesson plans or curriculum models, and the participants doing the gallery walk are familiar with the content and will want and need the time to really read and understand what is being displayed.

To increase the interaction with the audience, participants who do the gallery walk can be encouraged to make comments on sticky notes and leave them on the artifacts. This is a way to give positive feedback and for the teams to incorporate the ideas and suggestions of their colleagues. Model what is appropriate feedback: constructive and specific ideas that help teams move forward.

A Gallery Walk is a natural application for the classroom and can be used to display the work for the whole school. To heighten the complexity, a class might design their artifacts to be viewed by a younger class that is working on a similar subject. This vertical integration of the curriculum is a powerful way to help students understand what is meant by a connected curriculum.

MORPH GRID IV: FACILITATING GROUP WORK

Whole Group Strategy 11. Birthday Line Up

Explanation (What it is!)

As an energizing way to create new groups, ask the participants to line up according to their birth dates, beginning with one as January. The fun part is that they cannot talk to each other as they figure out the standings. Once the movement and gyrations have ended, group the participants by making the first two or three a new small group, and continue designating groupings along the line. Then, send them to a new spot to do their next task.

Application (When to use it!)

A constant challenge for the staff developer is finding new and better ways to change the composition of the groups. The benefits of changing up the groups far outweigh any negative feedback that participants may communicate, either verbally or with their body language. The *Birthday Line Up* does this for you, and when working with familiar staff members, there generally are pleasant surprises as colleagues realize they have similar birthdays.

Elaboration (How to use it!)

Have the whole class line up in a circle around the room, and then explain the strategy, making clear where the month of January is, and direct them to find their place in the line.

By lining them up first, you increase the amount of movement so that participants don't move from a sitting position to their spot in the line. Part of the energy created with the Birthday Line Up is when the students discover how they have to differentiate themselves and how they have to do it silently.

MORPH GRID IV: FACILITATING GROUP WORK

Whole Group Strategy 12. Puzzle Building

Explanation (What it is!)

An unusual way to get the group to mix and match is to have them solve a puzzle of sorts. In this type of activity, each member has a piece of the puzzle and they all move about as they figure out where the puzzle pieces need to go to form the whole.

Application (When to use it!)

Many active strategies designed for the adult learner are described as ice breakers or team builders, but because staff developers work with classroom teachers, the most pragmatic and practical of any adult learners, rigorous content should be embedded into every strategy.

Puzzle Building is fun and exciting for the participants, but they may gain deeper understanding of the topic of the day if the puzzle they put together somehow supports the learning goals of the workshop.

Elaboration (How to use it!)

One example of this uses the picture book called *Zoom!* In this activity, each participant receives a page from the book, and then, without having seen the original version, they are asked to put the book back together again. The trick is that they must solve the puzzle in silence. It is really quite fun, and it is surprising how well groups do with this activity. Naturally, any number of puzzles can be utilized to vary or customize this activity to the topic under focus.

MORPH GRID IV: FACILITATING GROUP WORK

Small Group Strategy 1. TTYPA . . . (Turn to Your Partner and . . .)

Explanation (What it is!)

TTYPA . . . is one of the easiest and most versatile interaction tactics known to man. It simply asks the participants to "turn to your partner and . . . tell them what they just said," or "turn to your partner and . . . give an example," or "turn to your partner and . . . agree or disagree with the statement."

While you might add *shoulder partner* or *elbow partner,* it is always a quick way to get a speedy interactive moment. More specifically, it is a team facilitation piece because it requires the participants to participate in the middle of a lecture, talk, or viewing.

Application (When to use it!)

When facilitating small groups, special attention should be paid to how many people are really talking. A great opportunity to use the TTYPA . . . is when there are six people at a table and five are listening to one speak. Before encouraging them to discuss a topic, structure the interaction by saying, "Turn to your partner and tell them. . . ."

When beginning a presentation, and before you sample the room for input about the topic of the day, instead of asking the whole group a question, which might elicit awkward silence or a response from one or two people, ask that same question of a small group. Before they can answer, say "Turn to your partner and tell them how you would answer this question. . . ." After they have talked for a couple of minutes, ask for input from the whole class. The responses you receive will be more elaborate and well-thought out than if you had simply asked your question of the whole group.

Take time to reflect on the strategy with the group, pointing out how the TTYPA . . . strategy allows the class to make sense of the question with a partner, to engage in cognitive rehearsal.

Elaboration (How to use it!)

When telling participants to Turn To Your Partner and . . . , remember to make it complex so that it is engaging. Instead of saying, "Turn to your partner and tell them what you know about differentiated instruction," it is better to say, "Turn to your partner and tell them how you differentiate instruction and why."

This higher-level question promotes conversation and critical thinking, and when it comes time to sample answers from the whole group, the responses will be that much richer.

MORPH GRID IV: FACILITATING GROUP WORK

Small Group Strategy 2. The Three Musketeers

Explanation (What it is!)

The Three Musketeers is for fast group formations of three. Ask each person to raise one hand and find two others to form a teepee of sorts with their hands. Then, once they have a threesome, instruct them to put their hands down and introduce themselves to the group, or say hello to their new partners.

Now, as the facilitator, you have new teams to do the next task or interaction. Have them work together as a team, and revisit this group throughout the workshop by having them return to their Three Musketeers group for various debriefings or reflections. Of course, you could do this same kind of new grouping with twos and call it *Tweedle Dee and Tweedle Dum.* If you need four in a group, call it the *Four Compass Points* or a *Four Poster* [Bed implied], and do a similar activity.

Application (When to use it!)

At the beginning of a training, after the introduction of the subject, and after the participants have been sitting for 20 minutes, their blood settles in their feet and in their seat. Getting them up and moving around with The Three Musketeers will increase the blood flow to the brain for better attention and cognition.

Revisit The Three Musketeers after break or after lunch as an easy way to keep the participants up and moving.

Elaboration (How to use it!)

When reassembling The Three Musketeers after the initial interaction, remind the participants that it is their spatial memory system that will help them find their partners from earlier in the training. Tell them, "Just go to your previous place in the room and your Musketeer partners will show up."

All learning is enhanced by the questions we ask, and this is also true when facilitating small groups. An effective way to scaffold The Three Musketeers is to have them discuss and then each share three things that they know about teaching the reluctant learner. Then, get the whole class's attention and direct The Three Musketeers to consider all of the responses in their threesome and summarize them into three bullets. Finally, before sharing examples, ask them to pick their top bullet point.

Help make clear what you have modeled for the teachers by "sharing the why" of the metacognitive conversation that was just modeled: the sharing of ideas, collaborative decision-making, and summarization and ranking of the top three. Identify that the groups have used three higher order thinking skills during the interaction. Those skills are decision-making, summarizing, and ranking.

MORPH GRID IV: FACILITATING GROUP WORK

Small Group Strategy 3. ABC Graffiti

Explanation (What it is!)

ABC Graffiti is the ultimate advanced organizer because it calls for 26 responses, instead of the usual small number. Have participants use poster paper and line up the alphabet in two columns on the paper. Then, assign a target word for each group or one word for the entire group. Give them about three minutes to complete the ABC format, and then count the number of responses they were able to produce. Remind them that they do not need to follow the alphabetical order but, rather, they can slot words on the chart as they occur to them. This makes a great vocabulary development or concept development activity in the classroom or in the staff room.

Then, ask the teams to circle the three best words—the words that most represent the target word. In this way, you are requiring the groups to critically look at the brainstorm of words and rank the best. This is very different from the original brainstorm of ideas. One calls for creative or generative thinking, while the other calls for analytical or critical thinking.

Application (When to use it!)

The ABC Graffiti is a great strategy that creates authentic emotional energy in the staffroom and should be used after the participants have been sitting for 15 to 20 minutes. When used early in a training, this strategy is a great way to *unpack,* or help define, an abstract word or key concept.

Elaboration (How to use it!)

After the teams have their papers ready, the alphabet on the paper, and an empty box at the top of the page, give them clear instructions before you reveal the word at the top of the page. This builds the anticipation and also keeps the teams from beginning before you have started the clock. The ABC Graffiti artifacts can be displayed around the room to model a word wall that shows what the vocabulary is of the participants on this subject.

A way to heighten the ABC Graffiti is to assign the role of the "Traveling Reporter" or "The Spy." Make very clear that the spy can go around to other tables and steal ideas but only when you, the instructor, allow it. This models a way to keep the groups at the same pace because no team gets too far ahead or too far behind.

After the three minute time is up, by show of hands, see how many letters the teams have completed. Have them put their score in the middle of the paper and then take them to the second step (finding the top three words in their list).

MORPH GRID IV: FACILITATING GROUP WORK

Small Group Strategy 4. Four-Fold Concept Development

Explanation (What it is!)

Use this four-step process to unpack a vocabulary word or a high-frequency concept, such as *collaboration,* or *organization,* or *facilitation.* Have table teams work on a poster paper that has been folded into four corner sections. Label them as follows:

Top left—List

Top Right—Rank

Bottom Left—Compare

Bottom Right—Illustrate

Then, have them fold the paper into four corners again, and fold the creased corners over into a small triangle. Have them open the paper and find the diamond shape in the middle of the page. Have them put the target word in the diamond: *consensus,* or *compromise,* or *competitor.* Using the four labels, move through the unpacking activity:

List—Brainstorm 20 to 30 synonyms or phrases

Rank—Select the three best words

Compare—Use this analogy: _____ is like _____ because both _____.

Illustrate—Draw a picture to illustrate your analogy

After completing the poster format, facilitate by sampling and sharing.

Application (When to use it!)

Like the ABC Graffiti, the *Four-Fold Concept Development* strategy is a way to dig deeper into a concept or idea using an engaging cooperative structure. Done correctly, the Four-Fold takes time but is very high energy, so plan to use it after lunch or late in the morning.

Elaboration (How to use it!)

This strategy takes time to scaffold; begin with the timed brainstorm, have them count their words, and tally who had the most. Next, have them rank the top three from their brainstorm. At this point, have the reporters from each group stand and form a half circle in front of the room. Have them read off just their top word, and go around the teams and then back to the first person who reads their next word until all of the top three words have been read aloud in an echo chorus. Direct the audience to listen for words that are mentioned many times and words that are unique. This models a way to develop active listening in the classroom.

Then, have the reporters return to their tables and take them to the analogy. When the groups have their analogy and are working on the comparison, move around the room and let them know that someone in the group will be the artist and illustrate the concrete idea they have as a comparison.

MORPH GRID IV: FACILITATING GROUP WORK

Small Group Strategy 5. Cooperative Learning Tear Share

Explanation (What it is!)

Cooperative Learning Group

Organize teams of four, seat them in chairs that are pulled away from the desk and arranged so they face each other, and have them count off 1, 2, 3, and 4. Then, have them fold a small paper into four corner sections and number them from one to four. They will copy four prepared questions in the four sections before they all read the designated piece and respond to all four questions. This part is done independently.

Tear and Share

After everyone in the group has completed the four questions, all four team members tear the sections apart and pass all the numbered sections to the appropriately numbered person. At this time, each of the four reads all four entries and summarizes the four papers to report back to the group. When everyone is ready, they do a round-robin sharing of the summaries.

Cautionary Note

You might need to facilitate the actual summarizing portion by discussing and modeling a summary instead of a complete rendition of all four responses. This can be an effective way to share an article or a piece of data because the facilitator can develop the four questions along the lines of Bloom's Taxonomy for more rigor.

Application (When to use it!)

The *Cooperative Learning Tear Share* is a great final strategy to help participants focus and apply what they have been actively learning all day. The Tear Share is intimate and engaging, and it allows the learners to see how much they have learned throughout the day.

Elaboration (How to use it!)

Make clear that each person has to have shared their summary before the group discusses or clarifies their responses. This way the pace of the strategy is maintained. If the groups discuss each summary as it is given, then the timing will be way off and some groups will be finished sharing when others are barely halfway done.

Process the Tear Share by asking the group to answer these questions about the strategy: "How does the Cooperative Learning Tear Share model interdependence? Engaged learning? Vested members?"

MORPH GRID IV: FACILITATING GROUP WORK

Small Group Strategy 6. Jigsaw/Expert Jigsaw

Explanation (What it is!)

There is a standard *jigsaw* of information or tasks, and then there is the *Expert Jigsaw*. The basic jigsaw is a simple division of labor, with each member preparing a part of the whole to share with the group. This can be quite effective when there is something that is a bit lengthy that you want to facilitate. The cooperative jigsaw will accommodate time efficiency and collaboration.

However, the Expert Jigsaw might be more appropriate if the information you want to facilitate sharing is complex or complicated in any way. Perhaps you have a task that would benefit from a deeper collaboration. This is when you should facilitate the Expert Jigsaw by forming subgroups for the preparation of the information or task.

In essence, there are two groupings: a basic group and a group of experts who pair up away from the basic group, prepare together, and then return to their respective basic groups to share the information or product. It might look like this:

Form Basic Group: 1, 2, 3

Meet in Expert Groups: 1, 1, 1, 2, 2, 2, 3, 3, 3

Reform Basic Group: 1, 2, 3

The cooperative jigsaw and Expert Jigsaw are foundational structures for the facilitation of group work.

Application (When to use it!)

The Expert Jigsaw is a strategy that can be done in two steps. A break can be called after the experts have come together and decided what to teach and how to teach it. It is a natural interruption in the flow of the day and will give the experts time to consider what materials they may need to teach their information.

After the break, direct the original groups to reassemble and begin the teaching round.

Elaboration (How to use it!)

Use the Expert Jigsaw with groups that need the challenge of applying what they know in the risk-taking role of peer teacher.

A key to an effective Expert Jigsaw is instructing the participants that when they teach what they have learned to their teammates, they have to use three of Gardner's (1983) Multiple Intelligences (MIs). In other words, to encourage good pedagogy, the experts will have to do more than just "tell them what they are supposed to know." Using at least three MIs in the teaching round is emotionally stimulating because of the challenge and risk involved. Facilitating the expert teams to diverge from what they would normally do bonds the team. Individuals are able to accomplish what they could never do on their own.

MORPH GRID IV: FACILITATING GROUP WORK

Small Group Strategy 7. Pyramid Game

Explanation (What it is!)

If you need a high-energy game format for the facilitation of a group meeting or session, there is no other strategy that will get the group energized like the *Pyramid Game.* Basically, you form AB pairs and ask them to place their chairs like a love seat, one facing front and the other facing back. Tell them that the A partners will begin by facing the screen, silently reading the target words you show, and will then give verbal clues to their partner so that the Bs will be able to discover the words on the list.

Prepare about six words in a category from the topic or concern under discussion, and proceed to show each one to the A partners. Then, reverse the pairs, and show another six words for the B partners to cue the A partners. It is a powerful strategy to stir up prior knowledge about the topic of the day.

Application (When to use it!)

The Pyramid Game is a simple strategy that models many of the key elements that make a successful professional development design. There is movement, changing of partners, fully engaged learners, rigorous challenge, and an authentic emotional release.

Use The Pyramid Game to review information that has just been taught in a more conventional lecture format or as a way to access prior knowledge at the beginning of a PD session.

Elaboration (How to use it!)

The Pyramid Game, as played on the popular TV game, is a race against the clock. Using the Pyramid Game with multiple pairs scattered throughout the staffroom is best done with a simple series of signals. With clear instructions, facilitate the teams from one set of words to the next. Instruct pairs to signal by putting their hand in the air once they get the word, just to signal to the presenter that they have guessed the word. Before putting up the next word, say "The next word is . . ." When about half the room has indicated that they have the answer, go to the next word. It is important that you keep everyone on pace by framing each word so the energy of the challenge is sustained for everyone in the room.

MORPH GRID IV: FACILITATING GROUP WORK

Small Group Strategy 8. AB Partners

Explanation (What it is!)

AB Partners are helpful to facilitate interaction by assigning different tasks to each partner and sharing the time in that way. It moves the interaction along more efficiently when time is short. For example, partner A might respond to the even-numbered questions the facilitator poses, while partner B responds to the odd-numbered questions. It is a simple strategy to help structure the time.

Application (When to use it!)

Small group interactions are powerful learning opportunities, but when adults are working in pairs the interactions can evolve into conversations that become so intense and engaging that it can affect the pace of the overall presentation. The AB Partners creates a framework that helps avoid this issue without losing any of the integrity of the content. For example, if the presenter is making a point by relating a personal story, a good strategy is to ask the audience to see if they can recall a similar story that they can tell to their partner. If there is an equal number of times that the partners can share, it makes for a good division of labor. With four or six main points to illustrate, it is natural to have partner A talk first, and then the next time they meet, partner B talks first.

Elaboration (How to use it!)

A key feature of successful AB Partners is to move the pairs away from any desk or table so that they are sitting knee to knee; this subtle change in the sitting arrangement makes a measurable difference in the level of engagement. Make clear to the audience that the AB Partners is a time management strategy in the active learning classroom. Keeping on pace is easier because the facilitators can interrupt interactions when it becomes clear that both partners are talking and the lead partner has probably finished their story.

The AB Partners strategy also fits when using text in the training; instead of having everyone read and comment, have partners A and B read the passage but have partner A respond, and then have them both read a passage and have only partner B respond.

MORPH GRID IV: FACILITATING GROUP WORK

Small Group Strategy 9. Think Pair Share

Explanation (What it is!)

Unlike a partner structure that merely dialogues, the *Think Pair Share* strategy requires that there are three distinct parts to the interaction:

Individual think time

Paired dialogue

A shared response

Think Pair Share can be used to process the results of an Agree/Disagree, as a response to a video, or to answer an essential question posed to at the beginning of a training.

The Think Pair Share is a natural transfer to classroom application that can be modified into a Write Pair Share, where everyone writes a response and then shares with a partner, and then partners come up with a shared written summary.

Application (When to use it!)

Think Pair Share, when used as part of a lecture, is a good way to hold the attention of the audience because they know that they will have a chance and an obligation to interact with the subject. Instead of calling on participants to respond to rhetorical questions that result in everyone listening to one person talk, Think Pair Share structures the interactions so that the entire class has a chance to talk and then to share with the whole class.

Elaboration (How to use it!)

For example, when the group is asked to respond to an agree or disagree statement, each person thinks about the statement individually, forming an opinion and a supporting argument. Then, the pair dialogues about their responses, and finally, they try to come to some shared opinion to announce to the group. It is a deeper interaction than simply talking with a partner.

Scaffold the Think Pair Share by asking the pairs to rank their ideas in order of importance or to summarize their answer into short bullet points. This adjustment to the structure of the answers adds complexity that reinforces the power of cooperative learning.

MORPH GRID IV: FACILITATING GROUP WORK

Small Group Strategy 10. High-Five Walk

Explanation (What it is!)

When the facilitator needs to move the group to renew the energy, the *High-Five Walk* is fun. As the saying goes, when you sit for 12 to 15 minutes, the blood settles in your feet and in your seat! By pumping your calf muscles six times, 25% of the blood will flow to the brain. This walk to music, high-fiving partners, is a lively activity to get that blood flowing.

Once the music stops, the High-Five partners of that moment become a new duo. Standing wherever he or she is, the facilitator poses a prompt for discussion in the partnerships. The topic can be anything that is related to the meeting focus. It will spark new conversations and new energy.

Application (When to use it!)

Good staff development begins and ends with a good design. In other words, the success or failure of most staff development can be predicted based on the amount of content the trainer includes in their day. Too much content takes time away from interactions and does not allow enough time for learning. And of course, it also does not allow enough time for teachers to consider how they can and will transfer the new ideas or strategies into the classroom. Unfortunately, this describes what passes for most professional development that classroom teachers are expected to endure.

Facilitating small group interactions with strategies such as the High-Five Walk is a perfect example of integrating music and movement to achieve what is a best practice in staff development: collegial interactions.

Use the High-Five Walk to infuse authentic energy into any training in order to punctuate a transition where you need to change partners. A high five is a great way to find new partners for AB Partners or the Pyramid Game.

Elaboration (How to use it!)

To really get the full effect of the High-Five Walk, make sure that the sound system is powerful enough to fill the training room with lively, upbeat music. Use a song that is familiar to the audience, perhaps a school fight song. Play the music long enough that the participants make at least two trips around the room. If you see common groups circling among themselves, decreasing the opportunity of unpredictable random partnerships, then step into the middle of the room and give them directions to mix it up. As soon as the music stops, whoever is the last person you high-fived is your partner.

MORPH GRID IV: FACILITATING GROUP WORK

Small Group Strategy 11. 3-2-1 Connect

Explanation (What it is!)

A wonderful pre- or postmeeting strategy, the *3-2-1 Connect* calls for partners to discuss three things:

3 Recalls

2 Insights or connections

1 Question

To make it more interactive, have the partners change after each interaction so that participants will have three different partners before they are finished. It is a great way to either reboot from the previous session or to recap and conclude the current session.

Application (When to use it!)

The 3-2-1 Connect, like any good reflective interaction, takes time to be truly effective. When used as a closing activity, include in the directions that participants should take their seat once they have finished their third conversation. This signals any who are still talking to find an end to their interaction. At this point, the facilitator can ask for examples of insights and connections that people discussed and can record them on a flip chart and then make a wrap up of the day by finding an overall connection between the examples and the goals of the training. The facilitator could also sample some of the questions and find common themes that will help with the design of a follow-up workshop.

If used at the beginning of a training, set the context for the audience that this strategy models the importance of accessing prior knowledge before any learning and how this strategy can be used in the classroom.

Elaboration (How to use it!)

Before beginning the 3-2-1 Connect, remind the participants that this strategy is about the power of reflective conversations with multiple partners. Also, the three different interactions model the three levels of information acquisition on Bloom's Taxonomy: recalls are knowledge/comprehension, insights and connections are analysis/application, and questions are synthesis/evaluation.

When facilitating the 3-2-1 Connect, listen to the groups to hear what they are saying and to keep them moving. This is a great opportunity to hear what they have learned and what they are going to take away from the training.

MORPH GRID IV: FACILITATING GROUP WORK

Small Group Strategy 12. Dial Information 4-1-1

Explanation (What it is!)

Dial Information 4-1-1 is an opening or closing strategy that calls for partner interactions. In pairs, participants discuss three things:

4 Memorable moments to share

1 Affirmed idea that feels good

1 New idea to commit to try

The participants take turns sharing four memorable moments; then, the partner shares the same. Then, they each share one affirmation, and finally, each shares one new idea to try.

Application (When to use it!)

The 4-1-1 is very similar to the 3-2-1, except that the 4-1-1 is a conversation between two people and doesn't involve moving after each interaction. The 4-1-1 is a wonderful way to begin a workshop because it allows time and structure for the participants to make connections to what they remember from previous trainings.

Elaboration (How to use it!)

The 4-1-1 can lead into intense conversations that are best managed with a signal that tells when participants should move from the moments to share, to an affirmed idea, and then to a new idea.

Possible signals could be musical cues or simply listing the steps of the 4-1-1 on a PowerPoint.

MORPH GRID IV: FACILITATING GROUP WORK

Individual Strategy 1. One-Minute Write

Explanation (What it is!)

The *One-Minute Write* is a marvelous structure to punctuate the facilitation of information. It is an individual task that is repeated with some goal setting and is then shared with a partner, so it has some complexity to it as a facilitated interaction.

Individuals are asked to get their pens poised for a one-minute write. They are given the topic and then timed for one minute exactly. At the end of one minute, the facilitator asks them to raise their pens to show they have stopped writing.

At that time, they are asked to count the number of words they wrote and to set a goal to improve their performance in the next One-Minute Write. They are then given a second topic and asked to write a timed one-minute piece again. This time, they count to see if they have achieved their goal. You can imagine how motivated they are to see if they have achieved a "personal best."

The One-Minute Write can be used with different kinds of goals besides the number of words or fluency of the writer. It can be used with strategies for problem solving, or intervention ideas, and so on. Play with it each time to see what works with your groups.

Application (When to use it!)

The One-Minute Write is an example of moving from active learning to engaged learning. Use this strategy after high-energy whole group interactions to bring focus to the subject and to allow the individual to process information in a solitary, mindful way. Modeling the appropriate time to use the One-Minute Write also helps classroom teachers see the power of a short, personally challenging task where the learner is measured against their best efforts rather than the level of their classmates.

Elaboration (How to use it!)

Have fun by building anticipation and making a big deal about the one-minute timer and that they are to write as fast as they can. Do not tell them the writing prompt until everyone knows the rules and is ready to write. If the topic of the One-Minute Write is revealed too early, many will begin to write before the time. This emphasizes the emotional element to the One-Minute Write that makes it more than a writing exercise.

MORPH GRID IV: FACILITATING GROUP WORK

Individual Strategy 2. Mediated Journal Entry

Explanation (What it is!)

A *Mediated Journal Entry* is a guided entry or a prompt for the writer to use as a catalyst. In the case of the mediated or guided journal entry, scaffold or prompt the entire entry to keep the writing flowing. An example of a Mediated Journal Entry is as follows:

1. Name someone you believe is a good problem solver (historical figure, fictional character, or personal acquaintance).

2. Tell two traits of your problem solver.

3. Describe someone who is not a good problem solver.

4. Tell how the two are different.

5. Write a closing sentence.

6. Give your piece a telling title.

Imagine how easy the prompts are to follow as the writer is literally carried along with the writing. After the participants have a moment to smooth out the piece, ask them to share with a partner, if willing to do so.

Application (When to use it!)

A Mediated Journal Entry is another focused writing strategy that provides a way for participants to learn using different modalities. When used early in a workshop, it helps to unpack an abstract concept or idea that will be the subject of the day. If the workshop is about reading strategies, then a Mediated Journal Entry about a literate person would allow reading strategies to be seen in the context of literacy and what a literate person is. A Mediated Journal Entry could be revisited at the end of the workshop to compare and contrast an earlier entry. Change the subject from "a literate person" to "a good reader" to see how much their thinking has changed and how they have incorporated new terminology.

Elaboration (How to use it!)

Instructions for the the Mediated Journal Entry should include that participants need to write in complete sentences. The journal entry should also be done with deliberate pacing, so that participants have time to write. After the last prompt, instruct participants to read back over their writing, smooth out any rough spots, and then share what they have written with a partner. Sample a couple in the big group, and finally, make a point to have participants reflect on how much writing they were able to accomplish in a short period of time.

MORPH GRID IV: FACILITATING GROUP WORK

Individual Strategy 3. Goal Setting

Explanation (What it is!)

Asking participants to set goals early on in the meeting or group interaction sets the tone for the rest of the work. Personal goal setting is a way to focus and anticipate what is to come. If the participants know where they want to go with the meeting, they are more likely to get there. In other words, if you don't know where you are going, how will you know when you get there?

Facilitate the writing and sharing of a short-term goal and a long-term goal. The short-term goal is what they might want to happen during the meeting time itself; the long-term goal is what they hope to take away from the meeting for later application or purposeful use.

Short Term Goal:

I hope to learn practical strategies for building consensus in my teams.

Long Term Goal:

I want to be able to take specific strategies back to my next team meeting to help me get more authentic participation.

Application (When to use it!)

Goal Setting is a very powerful strategy if used when rolling out a new initiative. By asking participants to set a goal for what they want to learn today (short term) and what they hope to learn at the end of the process (long term), you are setting the key conditions for transfer.

Take time for this strategy and add an element of interdependence by asking partners to share one of their goals. A key part of successful goal setting is making the goal public. When people go on the record about their intentions, they are more likely to meet their goal.

Elaboration (How to use it!)

Always model goal setting with a very specific example. For instance, a presenter who is introducing the new curriculum framework might say, "My short-term goal is to pare down this one-day training and develop a one-hour workshop that I can present as an after school inservice. And my long-term goal is that, by the end of the year, I will have a training manual in place using artifacts of schools I have visited throughout the year." This type of specific and time-bound goal setting will be what they come up with if that is what is modeled.

MORPH GRID IV: FACILITATING GROUP WORK

Individual Strategy 4. Mr. Parnes' Questions

Explanation (What it is!)

To facilitate learning that is relevant and meaningful to the participants, ask them to respond to the following two questions:

At the beginning of the session, after some initial input, ask the following:

"How does this connect to something you already know?"

Toward the end of the meeting, ask the following:

"How might you use this in the future?"

By facilitating these kinds of metacognitive reflections, you are forcing participants to make personally relevant connections. This gives weight and meaning to the topic at hand and facilitates a deeper understanding of the issues and their impact.

Application (When to use it!)

The use of video clips from popular movies or TV shows is a very common technique in the staff room, but many times the video seems to be played for entertainment and, as a result, an opportunity for learning can be lost. Before showing a video clip, pose Mr. Parnes' Questions, and after the video, have participants answer those two questions for each other. There will be many deep and relevant connections made and many serious ideas about application. Mr. Parnes' Questions can be used in a similar way as a response to a reading; a book study might use these two questions to guide their conversation throughout a whole year.

Elaboration (How to use it!)

For example, ask Mr. Parnes' Questions around a data meeting, at a faculty meeting on the new report cards, or during a discussion about the need for mentors, and so on. These questions truly facilitate personal commitment to the issues at hand. They take ideas from the abstract to the concrete.

Allow time for participants to talk, and when sampling connections made, consider writing the list on the whiteboard and then pointing out similarities and overlaps in the list. Moving to the second question, ask delving questions that challenge participants to be specific about applications that may spark ideas in others. Rich opportunities arise when well-posed questions are given time to inspire genius.

MORPH GRID IV: FACILITATING GROUP WORK

Individual Strategy 5. Letter of Commitment

Explanation (What it is!)

Asking participants to write a personal *Letter of Commitment* to action is a clever way to move the team members to application and transfer. By addressing a letter to themselves, and receiving that same letter at some later time, the participant is reminded, in an authentic way, of his or her earlier commitment.

Simply have participants write the letter near the end of the session and have them self-address an envelope. Then, collect the letters and save them until the timing seems right (e.g., the end of term, the beginning of the next term, or at a designated time during the semester). The arrival of the letter creates a buzz and a renewed focus to the commitment. It is really quite an effective strategy to facilitate active transfer and authentic applications.

Application (When to use it!)

When there may be a long period of time between meetings and to prepare participants for that next session, a Letter of Commitment from themselves will do a lot more to motivate them than another e-mail from the presenter. Coordinate the arrival of the letter with a significant period of time in the training schedule. Schedule the letter to arrive when the participants will need to see it the most, when it will do the most good.

Elaboration (How to use it!)

Model the Letter of Commitment and have a story prepared on how this strategy made a difference with your own learning journey.

Encourage participants to be specific in the letter and even add a personal touch, maybe a humorous aside that may seem corny but will make that person smile when they open the letter in the future. Have them use descriptive language that evokes just what they are feeling now, where they are sitting, and what they are thinking. The Letter of Commitment becomes a powerful reminder of how far the adult learner has come and what they have overcome.

MORPH GRID IV: FACILITATING GROUP WORK

Individual Strategy 6. Mrs. Potter's Questions

Explanation (What it is!)

Mrs. Potter is not Harry Potter's mom! Mrs. Potter is a wise old teacher who knew just the right questions to ask her students to get them thinking about their thinking and their work. She used the questions regularly, until they became part and parcel of her student interactions.

Basically, she asked her students four leading questions:

1. What were you trying to do?

2. What went well?

3. What would you do differently next time?

4. Do you need any help?

Now, it doesn't take a rocket scientist to see the value in this kind of personal examination. Imagine how helpful this kind of facilitation is when it follows whole group or small group work. *Mrs. Potter's Questions* cut to the chase:

What are you, the participant, taking away from this interaction?

What might you do to improve over the long run?

What kind of help do you need?

Application (When to use it!)

Mrs. Potter's Questions can be used as a simple self-assessment tool with cooperative groups. When teams finish ahead of the others, approach them and say, "As a group, answer Mrs. Potter's Questions."

When working with individuals, in a coaching or mentoring relationship, the hardest thing to do is to get the person being coached to focus on the positive. Mrs. Potter's Questions not only focus on the positive, they encourage the learner to consider what they may do next time.

Elaboration (How to use it!)

While this is a great way to process with a mentee, it is designed to be a self-reflecting tool. When using Mrs. Potter's Questions, emphasize how we want the adult learner to be reflective with others in conversation, but also to be reflective when thinking alone. Developing metacognitive thinking enables adults to learn without being taught.

MORPH GRID IV: FACILITATING GROUP WORK

Individual Strategy 7. Reflective Journals

Explanation (What it is!)

Reflection is the name of the game, and it often doesn't happen unless the leader facilitates it. Reflection is the down time when the participants think back on the interaction and their reaction to it. Journals provide a viable tool to facilitate reflection. Either used as a single journal entry or as a continuous journal over time, there are a variety of models that work. Here are six journals to consider:

1. Double Entry Journal: The first entry describes and the second entry reflects

2. Dialogue Journal: Two people move the journal back and forth

3. Response Journal: Responds to the activity, article, or input

4. Action Journal: Deliberate action steps planned out

5. On a Scale of 1 to 10: A forced ranking of the activity, article, task, or input

6. Electronic Journal: E-mail buddies use color-coded messages

Application (When to use it!)

Use the journals as an individual reflection strategy at the end or at the beginning of a session. Journal entries work well after the fact, of course, but journal sharing works at the start of the next session as a way to boot up the thoughts from the earlier session.

Elaboration (How to use it!)

One example of the Action Journal was written following a grade-level meeting that focused on low comprehension scores in the third grade.

After examining the data on our kids, I will plan more time on the comprehension strategy of visualization. Because I have so many English Language Learners, this is one of the comprehension microskills that I think is most helpful to enhance their understanding of what they are reading. I will devise ways to use visualizing skills, especially in content area reading in science, math, and social studies.

MORPH GRID IV: FACILITATING GROUP WORK

Individual Strategy 8. Ms. Poindexter's Questions

Explanation (What it is!)

Where did you get stuck?

How did you get unstuck?

These are two probing questions to ask when individuals are reflecting on a project or performance that is under way or has just been completed. Of course, this reflection is part of the process, the natural flow of things, for people to get stuck as their planned work unfolds. It is often enlightening to find out when, where, and how someone gets stuck. But the next concern is how one gets unstuck. In fact, sometimes more is learned from what did not work than from what did work. It's that examination that is quite revealing as individuals take a look at their thought processes and resourcefulness.

Application (When to use it!)

These are two powerful questions to ask when facilitating complex tasks, projects, assignments, or performances. Use *Ms. Poindexter's Questions* to add depth and richness to the meetings and sessions you facilitate. Honor the work that is done and the problem solving that is inherent in it. Don't be afraid to take this back to the classroom. It is a highly effective metacognitive question set to use with kids. It helps them understand that there is value in making mistakes and examining those missteps.

Elaboration (How to use it!)

After completing an action research study in her classroom, this middle school teacher shared the following comment, using Ms. Poindexter's Questions.

I think my greatest challenge, when I really got stuck, was after I had gathered a lot of classroom anecdotal data on math problem solving and was trying to make sense of it all. When I got "unstuck" was when I started coding my data—misread information, computation inaccuracies, did not show checked work, etc. That is when I really got a handle on things and realized how to set up my skill groups.

MORPH GRID IV: FACILITATING GROUP WORK

Individual Strategy 9. Personal Experience

Explanation (What it is!)

Personalizing an idea by targeting a personal experience that relates to it is a powerful metacognitive strategy. Relating new information or ideas to a personal experience is a way to make the learning relevant and meaningful. In this strategy, the facilitator simply asks participants to give a personal example to connect more intimately with the concepts.

"Can you find a personal example that helps to illustrate the concept of *conflict* and the strategies we discussed as possible reactions: ignore the situation, diffuse the anger, and escalate?"

Application (When to use it!)

This is a good individual strategy to use as an idea or concept is being introduced. It anchors the learning with that personal connection. It is one highly effective way to internalize the information in real and lasting ways. As people try to think of a real-life example, they literally move the theoretical or abstract ideas into concrete, meaningful understandings. It is a wonderful exercise to make meaning that sticks. It is no longer fuzzy. It becomes crystal clear to the learner.

Elaboration (How to use it!)

For example, if the topic under discussion is about the transfer and application of ideas, the personal connection might be a story of the time the participant applied an idea or strategy successfully. The more details given, the easier it is for the person to crystallize the true meaning of the concepts under scrutiny. It might sound like this:

When I learned about the "wait time strategy" of pausing 3 to 10 seconds after the teacher asks a question, I feel that I used it very effectively because I labeled it "think time" and cautioned the kids to "stop and think" before they responded.

It worked really well with my little ones, and I noticed two things: more frequent responses from formerly reticent students and fuller responses from all students who interacted. In the end, I believe that is the purpose of this wait time.

Notice the depth of understanding that is evidenced in personalizing the response. It definitely seems to help the reflective-practice process.

MORPH GRID IV: FACILITATING GROUP WORK

Individual Strategy 10. PMI—Plus! Minus! Interesting!

Explanation (What it is!)

The *PMI* or *Plus! Minus! Interesting!* is an Edward de Bono (1973) strategy that asks the learner to consider all sides of an issue. It is quite effective with adult learners because they are considering alternative solutions to a situation.

Plus—state all the positives that come to mind

Minus—examine all minuses that are possible

Interesting—note interesting aspects (not plus or minus)

In this case, while the facilitator may direct the PMI as a whole group activity, it is often more effective as a reflective piece that the individual does first and then shares with a partner. In this way, there is a greater opportunity for real dialogue. The PMI may also be used as a journal reflection and then shared the following session.

Application (When to use it!)

Use this PMI strategy whenever issues seem to be steaming up in the session. Take a moment, pause, and walk through a Plus! Minus! Interesting! question session. Also, to move toward consensus, the *minus* can be changed to a *delta*, which signals "What would you change?"

Elaboration (How to use it!)

An example of the PMI in action is using this strategy to discuss the various points of view regarding appropriate and specific interventions based on the data teachers are analyzing and interpreting. The PMI allows them to examine what the various outcomes might be—plus, minus, and interesting.

Data: Does not meet comprehension skills

Intervention: "Reciprocal teaching" strategy

(Summarize, Question, Clarify, Predict)

PLUS

The *plus* is that identified students will get a specific set of strategies proven to help comprehension (predict, question, read, and discuss).

MINUS

The *minus* is any drawback that might occur or unintended outcomes that could be a detriment to the anticipated goals.

INTERESTING

Things that are *interesting* are noticed but are not necessarily a plus or a minus. Perhaps they are just reflective thoughts to consider at another time.

MORPH GRID IV: FACILITATING GROUP WORK

Individual Strategy 11. Parking Lot

Explanation (What it is!)

The *Parking Lot* is a fairly well known strategy that skillful facilitators use to get feedback from the group. It is used as a "parking lot" for questions, concerns, and ideas that can be addressed more fully after the workshop or meeting, during breaks or lunch, or even on the next day.

Basically, there is a designated board for comments to be "parked" for later review. When it is used judiciously, it is an effective strategy. However, the facilitator must be sure to address the items on the board religiously, or the participants will feel that their ideas are not really valued. Once the Parking Lot is established, the facilitator must check it regularly and respond to it appropriately.

Application (When to use it!)

This is an effective tool for gathering immediate feedback from individuals on the concerns that are emerging for them. While it seems somewhat passive, it is really just an unobtrusive way of keeping the questions, concerns, and emerging issues at bay. It really is a management tool because it avoids interruptions and, sometimes, those unintended "bird walks" that take us away from the focus we want.

At the break, or during lunch, or even at the end of the day, the facilitator looks over the notes posted in the Parking Lot and decides how to best respond to each one. Sometimes, it will be to the entire group; other times it will be a one-on-one dialogue.

Elaboration (How to use it!)

Examples of Parking Lot Note. Some are content-focused, others are process-focused:

I need clarification on the term *differentiation!*	Is the ending time 3:00 PM?	What did you mean when you said "Standards for all, differentiation for each?"

MORPH GRID IV: FACILITATING GROUP WORK

Individual Strategy 12. Highlights/Insights

Explanation (What it is!)

This reflection strategy asks participants to process the session in two ways—cognitive reflections and metacognitive reflections. *Highlights* are the meat of the matter, while *insights* are the deep connections made about the central ideas.

Highlights—recap of points; content focused

Insights—reflective connections; personal thoughts

"One highlight for me was to understand that this 'pyramid of interventions' is not really new. We have been doing some of this with our flexible skills groupings in the differentiated instruction focus we have."

"An insight was that we have been looking at our data regularly, but we have not really targeted specific instructional intervention strategies. We have just gone back to our rooms and done more of the same. Although well-intentioned, it doesn't work very well, as evidenced by our unchanging data."

Application (When to use it!)

Facilitators use this strategy as a way to review the key content. They, then extend the comments to reflective insights or personal connections that the person is making. It is an effective discussion strategy that allows participants to fully digest and make relevant the input that has been shared.

Elaboration (How to use it!)

For example, a highlight might be that, "The key points of consensus-seeking are agreement, point by point, with concessions to make it palatable for all concerned."

Coupled with that, an insight might be that, "People can agree to disagree and still find consensus!" It may be the only plausible way to keep the process going and to proceed with the discussion or decision-making.

5

Applying Interactive Strategies

The One-Minute Lesson Planner

MORPH GRIDS

Classroom Applications Across the Disciplines

It is easy to see how readers can create their own versions of morph grids by inserting their own sets of strategies. It is also easy to see how teachers can use this morph grid idea in their classrooms. Here are a few examples that illustrate what teachers can do with this idea as they apply it to their classroom content.

Revisit: How the Morph Grids Work

The presenter can begin with this selected strategy (joke) as an opener to *capture* the attention of the group. Then, the presenter can captivate them with the "meat of the matter," using another strategy (cooperative learning task). Finally, the presenter can close using a *closer,* or final strategy (reflection). This process becomes quite clear as one actually looks at a morph grid and sees the array of items possible for selection.

It is said that creators of television comedies, dramatic series, and soap operas use a morph grid to keep their story lines changing from episode to episode. Thus, when an entirely new plot line develops, often introducing new characters, the story line literally morphs into something quite different.

Openers	Meat of the Matter—Middles	Closers
1. Strategy 1a	Strategy 1b	Strategy 1c—Reflection
2. Strategy 2a-Joke	Strategy 2b	Strategy 2c
3. Strategy 3a	Strategy 3b	Strategy 3c
4. Strategy 3a	Strategy 3b—CL Task	Strategy 4c
5. Strategy 3a	Strategy 3b	Strategy 5c
Etc.		

A final word on this morph grid is needed. Although the strategies are assigned to a column (openers, middles, closers), many strategies are interchangeable with those in other columns. An opener in one case might be used as a closer in another presentation. It really is up to the creativity and the risk-level the presenter is willing to take.

Revisit: How to Use Morph Grids Effectively

There are several options available for using the morph grids for the selection of the items. Some provide random approaches for selecting items from the three columns, while others simply choose tools and techniques more deliberately.

Making random choices is the preferred method; they often result in highly creative presentations. These random models, using forced choices, more often than not take the presenters into new territory, using tools and techniques that are a bit out of their comfort zone. Yet on the other hand, the deliberate choice of items in the three columns may provide the presenters with the most appropriate tools for the target presentation. Using either random or deliberate selection methods, here are a few ideas for selecting the various tools and techniques to mold a presentation.

Random Methods of Selection

1. Roll some dice and assign the numbers rolled to each column to make an entirely random group selection.

2. Use the last three digits of an individual's phone number and assign the appropriate numbers to the columns to select, again, random items.

3. Use a deck of cards, 1 through 9 and Jack = 10, Queen = 11, King = 12, Ace = Free choice.

4. Use the last three digits of an individual's Social Security number, or the first three digits of his or her date of birth.

Deliberate Methods of Selection

5. Have a designated team leader choose a number for each column.

6. Have various team members select an idea from each column.

7. Follow the order sequentially, until all ideas have been used once.

8. Choose two favorite strategies and one new strategy to move outside of the comfort zone.

Classroom Applications

Language Arts Teacher: Create a Story Grid

Headings of columns: Hero, Heroine, Villain, Setting, Plot, and Resolution

Hero	Heroine	Villain	Setting	Plot	Resolution
Lawyer	Doctor	Sibling	Shop	Kidnapping	Punishment
Salesman	Professor	Merchant	Street	Murder	Escape
Teacher	Electrician	Broker	Backyard	Argument	Cliff hanger
Webmaster	Editor	Accountant	Lakefront	Death	Happy
Dentist	Blogger	Author	High-rise	Surprise	Tragic
Musician	Life coach	Banker	House	Fight	Unresolved

Math Teacher: Create a Math Computation Grid

Headings of columns: Add, Subtract, Multiply, Divide, Greater by, and Equals

Add	Subtract	Multiply	Divide	Greater by	Equals
694	235	7	4	10	?
2	34	9	3	25	?
98	59	12	2	78	?
1,000	333	3	5	36	?
329	326	9	6	99	?
76	48	5	7	100	?

Biology Teacher: Create a Creature Grid

Headings of columns: Eyes, Body, Segments, Antennae, Legs, and Color

Eyes	Body	Segments	Antennae	Legs	Color
Small	Round	1	Big	2	Brown
Large	Square	2	Small	4	Black
Medium	Long	3	Spiked	6	Red
Bulging	Fat	4	Curled	8	Purple
Receded	Skinny	5	Long	0	Green
On the side	Triangular	6	Short	3	Gold

Consumer Sciences (Sewing) Teacher: Create a Garment (Blouse) Grid

Headings of columns: Fabric, Neckline, Bodice, Sleeves, Fasteners, and Decorations

Fabric	Neckline	Bodice	Sleeves	Fasteners	Decorations
Cotton	Jewel	Pleated	Long	Buttons	Sparkles
Silk	Collar	Plain	Short	Snaps	Leather
Wool	V-shaped	Lace	Sleeveless	Zippers	Strings
Linen	Plunging	Eyelet	3/4	Velcro	Appliqué
Polyester	Squared	Layered	Cuffed	Hooks	Lace
Satin	Round	Checkered	Slit	Ribbons	Fringe

Art Teacher: Create a Cartoon Character Grid (a la Mr. Potato Head)

Headings of columns: Head, Eyes, Nose, Mouth, Eyebrows, Ears, and Hair

Head	Eyes	Nose	Mouth	Eyebrows	Ears	Hair
Square	Squinty	Bulbous	Smiling	Bushy	Floppy	Ponytailed
Round	Big/round	Alpine	Sad	Pencil line	Stick out	Braided

Head	Eyes	Nose	Mouth	Eyebrows	Ears	Hair
Triangular	Slanted	Pug	Frowning	Arched	Sharp	Cowlick
Heart-shaped	Wide open	Flat	Full lips	Connected	Small	Bangs
Oval	Winking	Large nostrils	Heart lips	Rounded	Close to head	Curlicue
Cylindrical	Beady	Hook	Open	Hyphens	Medium	Straight up

Language Arts Teacher: Create a Grammar Grid

Headings of columns: Adverb, Verb, Adjective, Noun, Preposition, and Conjunction

Adverb	Verb	Adjective	Noun	Preposition	Conjunction
Gingerly	Carried	Colorful	Jar	Over	Yet
Spritely	Lifted	Pretty	Suitcase	Under	But
Lazily	Sorted	Worn	Chest	Above	However
Hurriedly	Walked	Old	Bike	Into	Therefore
Lovingly	Shifted	Ugly	Mirror	On	Without
Sloppily	Moved	New	Lamp	Beyond	While

Note: These can be developed into grid examples with 12 ideas for each column if you choose to roll two dice instead of one.

In Closing

The Morph Grids evolved over time as we listed our ideas over and over again, every time we planned a presentation. Eventually, we decided it would be smart to have a ready-made list of ideas so we could eliminate this time-consuming listing of ideas. Then, we realized that some activities were great openers, while others helped to make the presentation more interactive and involving, and still other strategies made for dynamic closures. Voila, the lists soon morphed into the morph grid idea of forced choices.

Appendix A

INDEX OF STRATEGIES

Auditory Tools

Jingle (II)

Joke (I)

Music (I)

Nursery Rhyme Summary (III)

Collaborative Tools

Card Storming (III)

Carousel (IV)

Carousel! Show and Tell! (III)

CL Pointer Game/Roles & Responsibilities (III)

Create a Contest (II)

D&D/Drop and Debrief (II)

E-mail/Text Buddies' Commitment (III)

Facts and Fun—Partner Introduction (III)

Give One! Get One! (II)

Inner and Outer Circle (I)

Inside/Outside Circles (IV)

Micro-Book Study (III)

Panel of Experts (III)

Personality Profile (II)

Points of the Compass (III)

Probe! Pause! Paraphrase! or PACTS (II)

Pyramid Game (IV)

Reader's Theater (I)

Role play (I)

TAGI—That's a Good Idea! (III)

Cooperative Learning Tools

2-4-8 Focus Interview (III/IV)

AB Partners (IV)

AB Pyramid Game (II)

Cooperative Learning Tear Share (I/IV)

High-Five Partner Walk/Music Stopper (III)

High-Five Walk (IV)

Human Graph (I/IV)

164

Jigsaw/Expert Jigsaw (IV)

Line Up Lanes (III)

People Search (III/IV)

Think Pair Share (IV)

The Three Musketeers (I/IV)

TTYPA . . . (IV)

TTYPA . . . Shoulder
Partner/Elbow Partner (III)

Energizer Tools

Energizers (II)

Energizers/Hurrahs/Cheers (IV)

Lighting and Sound Effects (I)

Prizes (II)

Surprise Guest (I)

Foldable Tools

Accordion Book or Z Book (II)

Fold-Over or Slip Slot Book (II)

Magic Book (I/IV)

Step Book (I)

Take Away Item (I)

Take Away Window (II)

The Tiny Transfer Book (IV)

Tri-Fold Brochure (III)

HOT Thinking Tools

Acronym (II)

Analogy (I)

Debate Contrasting
Statements (II)

Fat and Skinny
Questions (III)

List/Sort/Label (II)

Memory Pegs (III)

MI Grid (III)

Mystery (I)

Nursery Rhyme Summary (III)

Problem Based Learning (PBL)
Scenarios (II)

Puzzle Building (IV)

Q & A (III)

Rhetorical Questions (I)

The Three-Story Intellect (III)

Woven Questions (I)

Management Tools

Birthday Line Up (IV)

Deck of Cards (III)

Meet and Greet! Be Sweet! (II)

Parking Lot (IV)

Popcorn Out Ideas (II)

Shake and Break! I
Appreciate! (II)

Stack and Pack—I'll
Be Back! (II)

Reflective Tools

3-2-1 Reflect (I/IV)

Agree/Disagree—Think Pair Share (III)

Aha! Oh, No! (I)

Art Journal (II)

Bookmark Think About (II)

Circle Back to Beginning (I)

Dial 4-1-1 for Information (I)

Dial Information 4-1-1 (IV)

Double Entry Journal (III)

Five Minutes of Metacognition (III)

Highlights! Insights! (II)

Key Points (I)

Letter Journal Entry (III)

Mediated Journal Entry (III/IV)

Mr. Parnes' Questions (II/IV)

Mr. Pete's Questions and Cues (III)

Mrs. Potter's Questions (II/IV)

Ms. Poindexter's Questions (II/IV)

On a Scale of 1 to 10! Justify! (III)

One-Minute Write (IV)

Personal Experience (IV)

PMI—Plus! Minus! Interesting! (I/IV)

Punch Line/Circle Back Stories (III)

Quiz (III)

Quote (I)

Reflective Journals (IV)

Reflective Lead-In or Stem (I)

Reminder for Transfer (II)

Rhetorical Questions (I)

Signals—Red/Yellow/Green (III)

Story (I)

Vignettes (II)

Woven Questions (I)

Yellow Brick Road (I/IV)

Visual Tools

ABC Graffiti (II/IV)

Bridging Snapshots/Visual Metaphor (III)

Carousel! Show and Tell! (III)

Cartoon (I)

Costumes and Props (II)

Film Clip (I)

Four-Fold Concept Development (II/IV)

Gallery Walk (IV)

Graphic Organizer(I)

Images (I)

Metaphors and Similes (II)

Photo Story (II)

Picture Book (I)

Pie Chart (II)

PowerPoint (I)

Staircase (II)

T-Chart (III)

TV Character (I)

YouTube/Teacher Tube (II)

Appendix B

ENERGIZERS

Energize your group with movement. After 15 or 20 minutes of sitting, the blood settles in your feet and in your seat. Movement pumps blood into the brain for better cognition. Try these!

Cowboy Cheer

Put one finger in the air and circle it like a lasso as you say, "Yee-haw!"

Shine Your Halo

When the participants need an energizer, say "Shine your halo" while modeling the movement of running your fingers in a circle above your head. If you're looking for a way to get the participants to settle down, use the same cheer and ask, "Where are those angels? Shine your halo."

Olé! Olé! Olé!

Count with your fingers in the air as you say in Spanish, "Uno, dos, tres." Twirl around with your index finger in the air as you say, "Olé! Olé! Olé!"

Hamburger Cheer

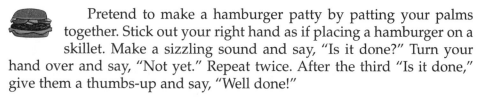

Pretend to make a hamburger patty by patting your palms together. Stick out your right hand as if placing a hamburger on a skillet. Make a sizzling sound and say, "Is it done?" Turn your hand over and say, "Not yet." Repeat twice. After the third "Is it done," give them a thumbs-up and say, "Well done!"

Sign Language Applause

Teach the participants how to applaud in sign language. They do so by raising both hands in the air and rotating them back and forth quickly.

A-W-E-S-O-M-E

Clap and sway as you cheer for your participants. "We're A-W-E (slight pause) S-O-M-E." Pretend to dust your shoulder with your fingernails like you're polishing them, one hand at a time, and say, "We're awesome, awesome." Now, open your arms outward one at a time and say, "To-tally!"

Firecracker

Hold your palms together in front of you as if praying. Make a sizzling sound (ssssss) as you wiggle your palms up in the air like a firecracker going off. Clap them above your head, then wiggle your fingers around and down like the sparkles coming from a firecracker. Make an "ahhhh" sound like a crowd watching a firecracker go off. Do a giant firecracker, a medium-sized firecracker, and a tiny firecracker.

Hip-Hip-Hooray!

The leader starts this cheer by slapping each hip as he or she says: "Hip, hip . . ." The participants all join in by shouting, "Hooray!" Repeat.

Pat Yourself on the Back

Have the participants pat themselves on the back as they say, "I'm good stuff." Next, have them pat their neighbor on the back as they say, "You're good stuff, too."

Lookin' Good

To compliment a participant, say "You are . . ." (make a clicking noise as you make a pretend mirror around your face and fluff your hair) " . . . lookin' good!"

Trucker Cheer

Tell the participants, "Grab your steering wheel." Make an "rrrrr" sound as you pretend to steer. Put your fist in the air and say, "Honk honk," as if pulling a horn. Next, put your fist by your mouth like it's a CB radio and say, "Good job, good buddy."

Cheese and Grater

 Hold up your left palm as you say, "Here's the grater." Make a fist with your right hand, and hold it up and say, "Here's the cheese." Pretend to scrape the cheese on the grater as you say, "You're great, great, great!"

Elvis Cheer

Tell the participants: "Turn up your collar; get out your microphone." Then swing the microphone around in circles, curl your lip like Elvis, and say together, "Thank you, thank you very much."

Fantastic

 Tell the participants, "Get out your spray bottle." Hold up one hand and pretend to spray. Say "You're psh, psh, psh . . ." (spray once for every "psh"). Hold up your other hand and pretend to wipe in circles over the liquid you just sprayed as you say, "Fan-tastic!"

Rattlesnake Cheer

 Put your palms together, and then wiggle them in front of you as you make a hissing (ssss) sound. Quickly stick your tongue in and out like a snake.

Saturday Night Fever

 Extend your right index finger in the air to the left of your body. Put your left hand on your hip. Move your right finger from the air to your side as you sing, "Ah, ah, ah, ah, we did a good job, we did a good job" (to the tune of "Stayin' Alive").

Seal of Approval

 Stiffen your arms; extend them in front of you, and cross them over each other. Clap them as you make a barking noise like a seal.

Harry Potter Cheer

 Tell the participants, "Get out your magic wand." Pretend to point your wand at various participants as you say, "You're psh, psh, psh, psh (point to a participant with each "psh"), Terrrr-ific."

A "Round" of Applause

 Clap in a circle to give the participants a "round" of applause.

Wow!

 To cheer for a participant without using words, put both hands on either side of your mouth with the pointer, middle, and ring fingers making a *w*. Open your mouth in a wide circle. This spells W-O-W!

Gold Star Class

 Tell your participants, "Get out your box (hold out one hand in a cupping shape), get out your star (pretend to get a star on one finger of the other hand), lick it, and put it on your forehead. You're all gold star participants!" This is a good way to help all the participants feel special.

I Like It!

When you're pleased with the way the participants have accomplished a task, get out of character and start singing: "That's the way, uh huh, uh huh, I like it, uh huh, uh huh. That's the way, uh huh, uh huh, I like it, uh huh, uh huh." Dance and sway as you sing.

References
and Resources

Backer, L., Deck, M., & McCallum, D. (1995). *The presenter's survival kit: It's a jungle out there.* St. Louis, MO: Mosby-Year Book.

Bellanca, J. (1990). *The cooperative think tank: Graphic organizers to teach thinking in the cooperative classroom.* Arlington Heights, IL: Skylight Training and Publishing.

Bellanca, J. (1995). *Designing professional development for change.* Arlington Heights, IL: SkyLight Training and Development.

Bellanca, J., & Fogarty, R. (2003). *Blueprints for achievement in the cooperative classroom* (2nd ed.). Thousand Oaks, CA: Corwin.

Bishop, C. H., & Wiese, K. (1938). *The five Chinese brothers.* New York: Putnam Juvenile.

Burke, K. (1997). *Designing professional portfolios for change.* Thousand Oaks, CA: Corwin.

Carle, E. (1986). *The very hungry caterpillar.* New York: Penguin Group USA.

Creech, S., & Bliss, H. (2003). *A fine, fine school.* New York: Harper Collins.

Cronin, D. (2000). *Click, clack, moo: Cows that type.* New York: Simon & Schuster.

de Bono, E. (1973). *Lateral thinking: Creative step by step.* New York: Harper Row.

Denmark, V., & Podsen, I. (2000). The mettle of a mentor. *Journal of Staff Development, 21*(4), 19–22.

Dietz, M. (1998). *Journals as frameworks for change.* Arlington Heights, IL: Skylight Training and Publishing.

Fogarty, R. (2000). *Ten things new teachers need to succeed* (2nd ed.). Thousand Oaks, CA: Corwin.

Fogarty, R. (2001a). *Differentiated learning: Different strokes for different folks.* Chicago: Fogarty & Associates.

Fogarty, R. (2001b). *Enhancing transfer.* Chicago: Fogarty & Associates.

Fogarty, R. (2001c). *Finding the time and the money for professional development.* Chicago: Fogarty & Associates.

Fogarty, R. (2001d). *Making sense of the research on the brain and learning.* Chicago: Fogarty & Associates.

Fogarty, R. (2001e). *A mentoring model for our teachers: Centers of pedagogy.* Chicago: Fogarty & Associates.

Fogarty, R. (2001f). Roots of change. *Journal of Staff Development, 21*(3), 34–36.

Fogarty, R. (2001g). *Student learning standards: A blessing in disguise.* Chicago: Fogarty & Associates.

Fogarty, R. (2001h). *Teachers make the difference: A framework of quality.* Chicago: Fogarty & Associates.

Fogarty, R. (2003). *A look at transfer: Seven strategies that work.* Chicago: Fogarty & Associates.

Fogarty, R., & Kerns, G. M. (2009). *Informative assessments: When it's not about a grade.* Thousand Oaks, CA: Corwin.

Fogarty, R., & Pete, B. (2003a). *Nine best practices that make the difference.* Thousand Oaks, CA: Corwin.

Fogarty, R., & Pete, B. (2003b). *Twelve brain principles that make the difference.* Thousand Oaks, CA: Corwin.

Fogarty, R., & Pete, B. (2004a). *The adult learner: Some things we know.* Thousand Oaks, CA: Corwin Press.

Fogarty, R., & Pete, B. (2004b). *A look at transfer: Seven strategies that work.* Thousand Oaks, CA: Corwin.

Fogarty, R., & Pete, B. (2005a). *Close the achievement gap: Simple strategies that work.* Thousand Oaks, CA: Corwin.

Fogarty, R., & Pete, B. (2005b). *How to differentiate learning: Curriculum, instruction, assessment.* Chicago: Fogarty & Associates.

Fogarty, R., & Pete, B. (2006). *From staff room to classroom: Planning and coaching professional learning.* Thousand Oaks, CA: Corwin.

Fogarty, R., & Stoehr, J. (1995). *Integrating curriculum with the multiple intelligences: Teams, themes, and threads.* Thousand Oaks, CA: Corwin.

Fullan, M. (1982). *The meaning of educational change.* New York: Teachers College.

Fullan, M., & Stiegelbauer, E. (1991). *The new meaning of educational change.* New York: Teachers College.

Gardner, H. (1983). *Frames of mind: The theory of multiple intelligences.* New York: Basic Books.

Garmston, R., & Wellman, B. (1992). *How to make presentations that teach and transfer.* Alexandria, VA: Association for Curriculum and Development.

Gladwell, M. (2002). *The tipping point: How little things can make a big difference.* New York: Back Bay Books.

Gousie, G. (1997, May). *Speaking with confidence.* Paper presented at the National Head Start Association, Boston, MA.

Grant, J., & Forsten, C. (1999). *If you're riding a horse and it dies, get off.* Peterborough, NH: Crystal Springs Books.

Hoffman, R. (1998). *I can see you naked: A fearless guide to making great presentations.* New York: Andrews & McMeel.

Hughes, P. (Ed.). (1991). *Teachers in society: Teachers' professional development.* Victoria: Australian Council for Educational Research.

Johnson, D. W., Johnson, R. T., & Holubec, E. J. (1986). *Circles of learning: Cooperation in the classroom.* Alexandria, VA: Association for Supervision and Curriculum Development.

Johnson, D. W., Johnson, R. T., & Holubec, E. J. (1998). *Cooperation in the classroom.* Edina, MN: Interaction Book.

Johnson, S. (1998). *Who moved my cheese?* New York: Putnam's Sons.

Joyce, B., & Showers, B. (2002). *Student achievement through staff development.* Alexandria, VA: Association for Supervision and Curriculum Development.

Kagan, S. (1989). Cooperation works. *Educational Leadership, 47*(4), 12–15.

Killion, J. (1999, Winter). Knowing when and how much to steer the ship. *Journal of Staff Development,* 59–60.

Knowles, M. (1973). *The adult learner: A neglected species.* Houston, TX: Gulf Professional.

Knowles, M., Holton, E., & Swanson, R. (1998). *The adult learner: The definitive classic in adult education and human resource development* (5th ed.). Woburn, MA: Butterworth-Heinemann.

Kraus, R., & Aruego, J. (1994). *Leo the late bloomer.* New York: Harper Collins.

Krupp, J. (1981). *Adult development: Implications for staff development.* Manchester, CT: Judy Erin Krupp.

Krupp, J. (1982). *The adult learner: A unique entity.* Manchester, CT: Judy Erin Krupp.

Lieberman, A. (Ed.). (1988). *Building a professional culture in schools.* New York: Teachers College Press.

Lieberman, A., & Miller, L. (2000). Teaching and teacher development: A synthesis for a new century. In R. S. Brandt (Ed.), *Education in a new era.* Alexandria, VA: Association for Supervision and Curriculum Development.

Little, J. W. (1975). *The power of organizational setting: School norms and staff development.* Paper adapted from final report to National Institute on Education, *School success and staff development: The role of staff development in urban desegregated schools*, 1981.

Moye, V. (1997). *Conditions that support transfer for change.* Arlington Heights, IL: Skylight Training and Publishing.

Parnes, S. (1975). *Aha insights into creative behavior.* Buffalo, NY: DOK.

Perkins, D., & Solomon, G. (1987). *Teaching for transfer in developing minds: A resource book for teaching thinking* (3rd ed.). Alexandria, VA: Association for Supervision and Curriculum Development.

Pete, B., & Sambo, C. (2004). *Data! Dialogue! Decisions! The data difference.* Thousand Oaks, CA: Corwin.

Pike, R., & Arch, D. (1997). *Dealing with difficult participants.* San Francisco: Jossey-Bass.

Piper, W., & Hauman, G. (1961). *The little engine that could.* New York: Platt & Munk.

Pitton, D. (2000). *Mentoring novice teachers: Fostering a dialogue process.* Arlington Heights, IL: Skylight Training and Publishing.

Radin, J. (1998, February). So, you want to be an educational consultant? *The School Administrator.* Retrieved June 2, 2006, from http://www.aasa.org/publications

Sarasan, S. (1982). *The culture of school and the problem of change* (2nd ed.). Boston: Allyn & Bacon.

Scearce, C. (1992). *100 ways to build teams.* Arlington Heights, IL: Skylight Training and Publishing.

Schmoker, M. (1996). *Results: The key to continuous school improvement.* Alexandria, VA: Association of Supervision and Curriculum Development.

Schmuck, R. (1997). *Practical action research for change.* Arlington Heights, IL: Skylight Training and Publishing.

Schmuck, R., & Schmuck, P. (1997). *Group processes in the classroom.* Madison, WI: Brown and Benchmark.

Sollman, C., Emmons, B., & Paolini, J. (2008). *Through the cracks.* Worchester, MA: Davis.

Sparks, D., & Hirsh, S. (1997). *A new vision for staff development.* Alexandria, VA: Association for Supervision and Curriculum Development.

Sparks, D., & Loucks-Horsley, S. (1990). *Five models of staff development.* Oxford, OH: National Staff Development Council.

Stern, N., & Payment, M. (1995). *101 stupid things trainers do to sabotage success.* Irvine, CA: Richard Chang Associates.

Sweeny, B. (2001). *Leading the teacher induction and mentoring program.* Arlington Heights, IL: Skylight Training and Publishing.

Tate, M. (2004). *Lessons learned: 20 instructional strategies that engage the adult mind.* Thousand Oaks, CA: Corwin.

Van Allsburg, C. (1984). *The polar express.* Boston: Houghton Mifflin.

Van Ekeren, G. (1994). *Speaker's sourcebook II: Quotes, stories and anecdotes for every occasion.* Paramus, NJ: Prentice Hall.

Wang, N., & Taraban, R. (1997). *Do learning strategies affect adults' transfer of learning?* (ERIC Document Reproduction Service No. ED413 419)

Whitaker, S. (2000). Informal, available, patient. *Journal of Staff Development, 21*(4), 23.

Williams, R. B. (1996, Winter). Four dimensions of the school change facilitator. *Journal of Staff Development,* 48–50.

Williams, R. B. (1996). *More than 50 ways to build team consensus* [Training Package]. Arlington Heights, IL: Skylight Training and Publishing.

Williams, R. B. (1997). *Twelve roles of the facilitator for school change.* Arlington Heights, IL: Skylight Training and Publishing.

Wohlsletter, P. (1997). *Organizing for successful school-based management.* Alexandria, VA: Association of Supervision and Curriculum Development.

Wong, H., & Wong, R. (1998). *How to be an effective teacher: The first days of school.* Mountain View, CA: Harry Wong.

Zemke, R., & Zemke, S. (1981, June). 30 things we know for sure about adult learning. *Training, the Magazine of Human Development,* 45–52.

Index

CORWIN
A SAGE Company

The Corwin logo—a raven striding across an open book—represents the union of courage and learning. Corwin is committed to improving education for all learners by publishing books and other professional development resources for those serving the field of PreK–12 education. By providing practical, hands-on materials, Corwin continues to carry out the promise of its motto: **"Helping Educators Do Their Work Better."**